The Body Is

a Clear Place

and Other

Statements

on Dance

THE BODY IS A CLEAR PLACE

and Other Statements on Dance

by Erick Hawkins

Foreword by Alan Kriegsman

A Dance Horizons Book
Princeton Book Company, Publishers
Princeton, NJ

Cover photo of Erick Hawkins by Joe Kirkish in *Geography at Noon*, 1964.
Back cover photo of the author by Joan Tedeschi. Copyright © 1992.
Erick Hawkins in *Trailbreaker*, 1940. Photo by Barbara Morgan.
Erick Hawkins in *Free State—Kansas*, 1940. Photo by Barbara Morgan.
Erick Hawkins in *Yankee Bluebritches*, 1940. Photo by Barbara Morgan.
Erick Hawkins in *Here and Now With Watchers*, 1957. Photo by A. John Geraci.
Erick Hawkins in "Pine Tree" from *8 Clear Places*, 1960. Photo by Dan Kramer.
Erick Hawkins and Lucia Dlugoszewski in *Geography at Noon*, 1964. Photo by Michael Avedon.
Erick Hawkins in "Thunder" from *Black Lake*, 1969. Photo by Ted Yaple.
Erick Hawkins as John Brown in *God's Angry Man*, 1945. Photo by Michael Avedon.
Erick Hawkins in *Naked Leopard*, 1966. Photo by Michael Avedon.
Erick Hawkins and Cynthia Reynolds in *Death Is a Hunter*, 1986. Photo by Martha Swope. Copyright © 1986 Martha Swope.
Erick Hawkins, Randy Howard, James Reedy, and Mark Wisniewski in *The Joshua Tree, Or Three Outlaws*, 1984. Photo by David Fullard.
Erick Hawkins in *Ahab*, 1986. Photo by Peter Papadopoulos.

A Dance Horizons Book
Princeton Book Company, Publishers
P.O. Box 57
Pennington, NJ 08534

Cover design by Deirdre Sheean
Interior design by Meg Davis
Typesetting by Peirce Graphic Services, Inc.

Library of Congress Cataloging-in-Publication Data

Hawkins, Erick.
  The body is a clear place and other statements on dance / Erick Hawkins.
    p. cm.
  Includes bibliographical references.
  ISBN 0-87127-166-4 (pbk.)
  1. Dancing—Philosophy. 2. Modern dance—Philosophy.
I. Title.
GV1588.3.H39 1992
792.8—dc20   91-50930

Contents

Foreword/ Alan Kriegsman

E rick Hawkins—eighty-two at the time of this writing—has
long since earned an exalted place in the history of the arts, as
a masterful and influential teacher, as a performer of extraordinary magnetism and power, and as the maker of a still-growing
body of dance theater works of indelible originality, beauty and
poetic incandescence. Those who have been privileged to see him
dancing will recognize in his writings the same qualities of granitic
strength, impassioned conviction and clear-eyed certitude of purpose, as well as an occasional ornery streak, that ennoble his
performances. Those who know his dances will find a rational and
reflective basis for the technique they embody, for their pervasive,
unsentimental and reverent approach to nature (including human
nature, inseparable, in Hawkins' eyes, from the biological and
physical continuum which is the world), for their magical sense of
timelessness (or rather, the eternity of the instant), and for their
intuitive, sublime poetics.

The mind of the creative artist as revealed in these essays is a
mirror of his creations, which reflects both more and less than the
whole story. Less, in the sense that the dance works themselves are
wholly autonomous, speak for themselves, and communicate in a
way profoundly beyond the reach of words, requiring neither
"explanation" nor commentary for appreciation of their value.
More, in the sense that the author herein reveals relevant things that
the works do not contain or at most imply—such matters as
inspiration, motivation, personal and historical background, theoretical precepts, and philosophical perspective.

There's no need here to rehearse in detail the facts and
circumstances of Hawkins' life, but it is important to underscore the
uniqueness of his career, historic situation and aesthetic stance. The
data of his biography are amply related elsewhere—his Colorado
boyhood, including the contact with Native American cultures that
made so deep and consequential an impression; his immersion in
classical antiquity at Harvard, where Lincoln Kirstein was among
his classmates; his admiration of and subsequent studies with the
German expressionist soloist Harald Kreutzberg; his enrollment in

the inaugural class of George Balanchine's School of American Ballet and performances with Balanchine's earliest American entourages; his first choreographic effort, for Ballet Caravan, spurred by the encouragement of Kirstein and Balanchine; his meeting with Martha Graham at Bennington, and his ensuing long, complex involvement, both personal and artistic, with her as her first male dancer, counselor, guide, partner, lover and, for a brief period, husband; the establishment, in 1951, of his own school, company and artistic voice; his unremitting insistence on the use of newly created music and live performance, and his prodigiously fruitful collaborations both with composers Lucia Dlugoszewski, Virgil Thomson, Alan Hovhaness, Lou Harrison, Dorrance Stalvey, David Diamond and Ge Gan-ru, and with such visual artists as Isamu Noguchi, Ralph Dorazio, Robert Motherwell, Helen Frankenthaler and Ralph Lee.

One of the things that stands out from this remarkable panorama is Hawkins' key relationships with the pair of certifiable dance giants of this age—Balanchine and Graham. As he freely acknowledges, Hawkins owes much to each. In the quintessential tradition of modern dance, though, he rebelled quite thoroughly from both, recalling Steve Paxton's ingenious witticism, "If we don't do what our predecessors did, we're doing what they did." The vision and practice of dance that Hawkins has forged, however, is neither a blend or a compromise between the approaches of Graham and Balanchine, but something as distant from either as they are from each other. It is a dance metaphysics that rests neither on psychology nor plot, nor social or political agendas. It is also equally remote from movement conceived solely as pure form or musical analogue—form, yes, pure, yes, but, in Clive Bell's resonant phrase, "significant form," form that aims from the start to be puissantly expressive. And in Hawkins' case, the locus of that expression is almost invariably the confluence of nature and spirit.

The essays that follow are not memoirs, nor are they codified theory, didactic tracts or anecdotal musings, though they partake of some qualities of each category. Rather, they are essays—articulate meditations that disclose the characteristic flow of their author's independent, willful, pungent, wide-ranging, unorthodox and flinty intellect. In "Art in Its Second Function," there is an elucidation of the interdependence of form and function central to Hawkins' art, and such observations as

> Perhaps the theatre, even the dance theatre, is the church of our time. At its most profound, it embodies the ritual of an inner life, rather than portraying the husk of an outer life. Every society needs rich metaphors of the collective insights that a culture lives by.

"The Body Is a Clear Place" argues for Hawkins' concept of free, as opposed to bound, flow as a paramount goal of dance technique; "Questions and Answers" contains, among other things, a litany of traits the author equates with beauty in dance—"Dance that is violent clarity," "Dance that lets itself happen," "Dance that dedicatedly loves the pure fact of movement," as examples; in "Inmost Heaven," ranging over the theme of the gulf between the actual and the ideal in many realms, the author declares, "After I had been studying dance a while, I knew that I had to find the equivalent simplicity, clarity, directness, effortlessness, strippedness, in dance movement that I knew I liked in everything else." "The Rite in Theatre" celebrates the artistic essentiality of myth:

> Historically, the place in every culture or group where myth and rite are expressed is in the theatre, whether it is the ceremony of the Navajo medicine man; the Balinese Ramayana shadow plays; the Japanese Noh theatre; the Catholic mass; the New Mexican Penitentes' enactment of Calvary; Shakespeare; the medieval European mystery plays; or Athenian tragedy.

In "Modern Dance as a Voyage of Discovery"—which begins with the wonderful notion, "The most beautiful thing, the most exciting thing about modern dance is that nobody can define it"—Hawkins sounds this credo:

> I conceive of modern dance as a direction of the human spirit here in America in the making of art which cannot repeat, relive, rewarm, stand still, copy or revert or keep corpses alive.

"Dance as a Metaphor of Existence," on the broadest possible implications of dance aesthetics, includes the rueful aside, "In

America, there is still the feeling that art is something you can take or leave. But our sadness in the midst of plenty belies that idea." "The Principle of a Thing," a spirited defense of Hawkins' own points of aesthetic departure, dares to get down to basics in an exploration of the technical foundations of expressive movement.

Of course these are hints, merely. The essays, too, speak for themselves, and without further ado I invite you to the extravagant rewards and pleasures of reading them.

Preface/ Statement of Erick Hawkins

I would like to see pure fact occur in the art of dance and pure fact is the rebellious rediscovery of the innocence of the materials. Only when one has the innocence of the materials can there possibly be created the tender gesture which is the only real relationship of people to one another on stage.

I would like to see choreography of such immediacy that the dancer could momentarily resolve that baffling paradox of thought and action, and the naked beauty of real motionlessness would happen on stage.

I believe in the possibility of a choreography of such immediacy that time could be sensed in its most difficult and yet most haunting dimension, time sensed instant-by-instant, a kind of time freed from space.

Thus, dance in America today would be an art worthy of being experienced, watched, understood, appreciated, discussed, and criticized, on the level of the other mature arts—poetry, painting, sculpture, architecture, and music.

And it would be not only a mature art, but a really modern art! Thus, American dance would contribute its own unique insights to the new, exciting aesthetic principles of the other arts of today.

I would like to see dance as a modern art in America today, to realize that it is possible to explore movement in and for itself, to delight directly in the innocence of its own materials and its own being—more like the work of a Calder, a Miró, a Brancusi, a Tobey, a Varèse, an e.e. cummings, a Morris Graves—and realize it doesn't always have to revel in *sturm und drang* but rather in the pure fact of movement, which is our poetic experience of "now."

I would like today's dance to stop "interpreting" music, to stop its slavish dependence on music, whether "good" music or "bad," such as jazz. I would like to see dance challenge composers to write a live new music, written now for dance itself.

I would like to see our dance, as a modern art, throw away all its crutches, all its eclectic borrowings, and find its own deep physicality, its own sensuousness, its own passionate intensity. I would like dance to create its own theatre of pure fact, which is immediacy. I would like to see audiences know how to look not just with their eyes, but with their whole body, and look in time, instant-by-instant, and perhaps sense that ultimate innocence of pure movement or, even more astonishingly, pure motionlessness.

March 16, 1959

One/ The Rite in Theater

A talk by Erick Hawkins given before the National Theatre Conference at its annual convention, Hotel Picadilly, New York City, November 27, 1947.

I am a dancer. What I have to say today is an explanation, I think, of why the dance can play an important part at this special time in the total picture of service and preserving the world.

May I quote from an extraordinary speech made at the end of the war [World War II] in Washington by General G. B. Chisholm of Canada, a psychiatrist who was Director General of Medical Services of the Canadian Army. "So far in the history of the world there have never been enough mature people in the right places . . . people who were sufficiently free of the neurotic symptoms which make wars inevitable.

"The burden of inferiority, guilt and fear, commonly known as sin, lies at the root of this failure to mature successfully." Chisholm goes on to say that "the lowest common denominator of all civilizations and the only psychological force capable of producing these burdens is morality, the concept of right and wrong."

This is to say that the only basic prevention of war is the existence of a preponderance of individuals in the world who are mature, who are—in psychological terms—not at war with themselves. When the various components of the psyche are at war, or are not in balance, the individual cannot go forward into growth, into maturity, into allowing the life instinct (love) to triumph over the death instinct (hate, aggressiveness, destruction of others and self-destruction).

One might speak of this using Freud's terms, the super-ego, the ego and the id: heaven, earth, hell. Or from another point of view: if the conscious and unconscious of the individual psyche are not functioning in balance, one or the other being over-dominant and top-heavy, you find an inner civil war, which enlarged is civil war, as in Spain, or international war.

General Chisholm continues: "We are choosing now, perhaps passively, but inevitably, whether we shall be slaves of the next master-race or members of a world unity . . . At such a time is it not apparent to every serious student of any aspect of human living that events call upon him to manifest his particular kind of functional effort to preserve that very human society which has culminated in his peculiar privilege to pursue that truth?"

Our activity is in the theatre. If we were to ask what is the main and largest function of the theatre, what would we answer ourselves? Surely we would say it is not rationalism, preaching, teaching, propaganda. Those purposes can be served and used in the proper places: education, psychiatry, politics and intellectual and scientific research. The theatre is not a forum, nor a laboratory, nor slice-of-life photography, nor primarily entertainment.

No, the great function of the theatre is to present the myth.

Of the meaning of myth, Jung, the analytical psychologist, says: "Myths are first and foremost psychic manifestations that represent the nature of the psyche . . . The god or hero of the myth dwells nowhere else than in the psyche of man." Therefore, to speak in terms of the one great myth matrix: one might say that the myth is the representation of the inner psychic drama of every individual, is a representation of how the life instinct (growth, creativeness, love) must triumph over the death instinct (hate, destructiveness of others or of the self) so that the individual can travel the course of the sun, leaving the mother, the parents, in the sea, rising to his full powers of maturity at noonday and, relinquishing his heyday, sink with dignity and a sense of proper completion into the sea at the end, there to achieve immortality through children and works, making the night journey under the sea, to arise again, immortally, the next day.

Every event in human life is a reaching toward growth, unless that growth is thwarted. The attempt to achieve growth, the completion and integration of the total personality, has been the goal of all religions, no matter how much it might be perverted in time. The triumph of the death wish in actual suicide, neurosis or psychosis prevents the individual from completing the fully developed human cycle. At each stage of one's life, the life instincts must continually win out, or the human being is not ready to die. I would say that art in its important use—not the attenuated form we sometimes confuse with the term "art"—has been the external means of arriving at this inner integration.

Art that is only sensation or entertainment is only serving an inadequately conceived function and cheating us of the spiritual food we need to live. Somehow, the human soul has to have access to the deep, psychological patterns of growth. These patterns are accumulations, a collective result from the collective unconscious which each man inherits, as he inherits his physical body. Religion and art give him access to these patterns.

In essence, there is only the one theme, the one myth. The myth is the telling of the one image. The enactment of the myth is the rite, the doing of the myth, the dromenon, the drama. When I use the word "drama," do not think just of Greek drama. The event, the rite, is the same the world over. Theatre stems from rite.

Historically, the place in every culture or group where myth and rite are expressed is in the theatre, whether it is the ceremony of the Navajo medicine man; the Balinese Ramayana shadow plays; the Japanese Noh theatre; the Catholic Mass; the New Mexican Penitentes' enactment of Calvary; Shakespeare; the medieval European mystery plays; or Athenian tragedy.

To quote the poet Louise Bogan: "It is the rite which enables the individual to participate in the myth. The myth can be lived only through the rite." Whatever the historical state of development of the theatre in America today, to go too far from its origin—the dancing place where the rite is performed—is to forego its greatest power.

In a general way, what is the effect of rite on the spectator? The rite is a symbol of redemption. The individual's participation in the rite is almost a magical thing. How to explain it would be as hard as to explain how dreams can heal, as shown in the exacting study in the healing powers of dreams by John Ledyard in his book, *The Lady of the Hare*. The deep unconscious has to have a schema by which to live. It is as though the enactment of the rite is a beacon, a symbol, a mandala, the process of inner growth, balance and unity.

A quite extraordinary thing happened a few years ago. Most of you have probably seen Martha Graham perform her dance, "Lamentation," or have seen photographs of it. It is very simple, not long. A woman whom I know had seen her twelve-year-old boy killed in an auto accident. For years, she was not able to cry. Upon seeing Martha's dance, she wept.

One way of speaking of the rite is to call it by the Greek word *agon,* a struggle, not of any realistic behavior, but of the inner man. The self-destructiveness of any hero of myth and rite is one's own self-destructiveness. Terror and fear, Aristotle says, arises from recognition of one's own aggressive impulses. It occurs when the observer or participant of the rite witnesses prototypes of his own hate and destructiveness, often taking the form, through hubris, of self-destructiveness and a yielding to the death instinct, which I think, from what I know at this moment, must be postulated as part of every man.

Through witnessing the prototype in the myth or rite, or drama, the spectator feels his own death instincts come to consciousness and he can then control them.

The evocation of pity is the opposite tide. Pity is akin to love. The release of pity is the release of the life instinct and hence love. When the individual can love, he can live. The rite achieves this on a deep level of the unconscious, far below the rational. Our unconscious wish is to find in the art the triumph of life over death. The resurrection of the hero, by whatever process or whatever degree in the tragic myth, sets a deep pattern of hope and faith which heals in the dark.

In all the highly developed theatres of Oriental cultures, the actor and dancer is the same person. In some languages, there is no word to distinguish the actor from the dancer. That has been true in all primitive societies and presumably was true at one time in Athenian theatre.

The return of freedom of the human body in Western civilization determines the use of dance as the groundwork of the mature theatre of the future.

It is as though in this way, we could bring back into play the unconscious, directly through the body, and allow the intuition to find its balance against the present preponderance of the intellect and arrive at the whole man.

The element of rite and its primary instrument, dance, releases, I feel, the other components of theatre. The use of dance at once brings speech from off the street into the poetry of inner action. Dance obviously makes a real alliance with music in the theatre. Who has not been amused on going to a Broadway theatre to see some realistic play with interludes of salon music that Delmonico's dinner orchestra in 1905 would have been ashamed to play? It is impossible to connect realism with the inwardness of music.

The element of rite and dance frees the stage designer from remaining a Broadway interior decorator. What on earth kind of theatre results from bringing an assemblage of real furniture or duplication onto the stage? Only a boring one.

The attempt to find the sense of rite has already brought about results even in the design of the theatre itself. Arch Lauterer's[1] design for a dance stage at the armory for the Bennington School of Dance achieved an exciting three-dimensional dancing place, with simple means. Space itself is an element of design in modern choreography. Whoever saw Hanya Holm's theatre piece, "Trend," years ago with Lauterer's set, witnessed a fine example; or Martha Graham's "Primitive Mysteries," which is a danced rite or danced mandala; or her "Frontier," in which stage space is used to evoke the enormous sense of space on the American frontier; or Doris Humphrey's "New Dance" which made a great space architecture. Stemming from Isadora Duncan, the space of the dancing place of the rite even extends to the actual use of the body in modern dance—the third dimension, the use of the volume of the body, as compared with the essentially corseted proscenium-designed movement on the extensions of the body as exemplified in European ballet.

It is because of what is at stake that I feel the theatre today must regard itself as an art, if it is going to function in this wider design of contributing to the maturity of our people.

The European ballet, the historical development of dance in Europe over the last three hundred years, has its place. But the attempt, beginning in 1934, to introduce the European ballet into the stream of American theatre was a great and gratuitous mistake. Part of the motivation was commercial, but some was simply part and parcel of the same Beaux Arts taste that, at an earlier time, imported for us the Metropolitan Museum's architecture.

For the European ballet, with its so-called nineteenth century aesthetic and technique, to be grafted onto our American art stock, would be the equivalent of the Greek revival of a hundred or so years ago which put Greek columns in front of our banks, Widener Libraries (at Harvard University), and even our memorial to

Lincoln—so much deadwood for our creative architecture to cart off.

Granting to any degree the premise that today, of all times, we need the theatre to help its communicants toward individual spiritual maturity, it is not a misstatement to say that the European ballet, as it developed historically, set a premium on adolescence which it had not relinquished to any noticeable degree. It confuses dance with the body. The dance, as art, does not dance the body. It dances the soul, the inner man.

It appears significant to me that one of the outstanding ballet choreographers of modern times, Michel Fokine, honored and theoretically successful, produced as the last work of his maturity a piece called "Bluebeard." Those of you who saw it know what I mean.[2]

The idea that American dance could use the European technique and psychology as a basic stock appears false to me. There comes a time in a nation's culture, as in an individual's life, that he must do his own work and speak out of his own core. No matter how humble the modern American dance may be, it knows where it is going. At this moment, I would say that direction, not speed, counts.

Exactly what form the myth and its theatrical embodiment, the rite, will take in our theatre, I wouldn't presume to say. But by our psychological constitution, men need symbols of integration in the inner drama (life) today more than ever. The artists' job is to find those symbols for use, just as the physicist, the statesman, the economist, the psychiatrist serve their function in serving their fellows. The need must be recognized and the challenge accepted.

I do not see why it is necessary to deny ourselves great works of art in the theatre by the limitation of our image of what it can be. Why should there not be in the field of dance and of theatre powerful conceptions and expressions comparable to Picasso's "Guernica" or Bartók's "Concerto for Orchestra" or T.S. Eliot's "Wasteland"? Why only emphasis on adolescence, charm, virtuosity, ingenuity, cleverness, chic and nostalgia? Picasso, in "Guernica," goes back a long way for his symbols and for his outlines. But essentially, he has delineated a myth in painting. It is not a question of going back to mythology—a specific set of myths of one people or time. It is a question of telling the myth and the great rite of growth from his own maturity, because that is what each individual needs from the artist to help him live.

The artist is a priest, and as Coomaraswamy says, "We should be producing Mystery Plays." Indeed, I think it was because unconsciously I felt so strongly the personal need of the rite that I chose to become a dancer.

Two/ Theatre Structure for a New Dance Poetry

Notes written during the early period of composition of "Here and Now With Watchers," outlining the choreographer's aesthetic aims. The first performance was on November 24, 1957, at Hunter Playhouse in New York. This essay was then published in Castalia, *a semiannual magazine of literature and the arts, Fall 1961. Antioch College, Yellow Springs, Ohio.*

Each live thing in itself has its own level of poetry, but when two live things are juxtaposed, a third level of poetry exists between them. (Of course I use the word "poetry" to mean that deep, exciting center of all things that we in the West have often termed "spirit" and that perhaps the Japanese have called "suchness" or that the Chinese have equated with the character "ch'i." (Another way of saying it is to call poetry "the secret life of each and all the arts.") In any case, I feel that this thing which I have now called poetry is the most important thing in the world; its levels are limitless, and to deny any one level or any minutest facet is to deny the whole world.

My more and more evolving consciousness of this most important thing in the world has brought the idea of a whole new work to me. This would be a work of deep juxtapositions, or even collaboration as a material in itself, of the everythingness of everything and every thing.

Of course just to work in movement within Western culture is to complete some of the everythingness in our moment of the world. Since the time of Sappho we have enchanted the world. Color has constantly opened us. Sound has dropped many times into our depths. But how we have forgotten human eyes *that move;* or live fingers with *three* wonderful joints; our exquisite knees; our spines that wriggle and grow with meaning; the magic aliveness where our legs nestle into the body; and even the head, not thinking life into a standstill, but feeling life into existence. I would like to help us remember.

Creating a new theatre art live enough to admit all the levels of poetry is still everyone's unknown country. Our drama has not body to remind our body, not flesh to awaken our flesh, only the spoken word for its poetry.

Perhaps in dance the foot has spoken, but in its shoes and toe shoes it is a foot ours could never be. I want to remind us of feet deliciously, nakedly belonging to us.

There is an ancient aesthetic duel between life and art and I do not propose any solution, because I deny the duel just as I deny the duel between men and women, and this dance will remind me of this denial.

All over the world, creating heals; and living is. But when living isn't, art infects. And what is healing but reminding us that we are.

In Hindu mythology the role of the dragon is one waiting to destroy every new conclusion by being its opposite. It would be to slay the dragon by creating a dance of the everythingness of me at this now of my being.

I have planned a structure of dovetailing solos and duets, for a man and a woman, consisting of thirteen units with thirteen changes of costume which can be made almost instantaneously. The total work would run about an hour and fifteen minutes and each unit would be a different length from all the others so that the whole would present in the time structure itself a poetry of lengths. The choreography would be created first in silence so that in no way would it deny itself by using the music as the crutch it has become for most dance. Also, the form deeply inherent to movement would have a chance to discover itself since we have no tradition of form for movement in the West and too often the temptation has been to borrow musical form.

After the dance is composed, music would be commissioned in which the composer (Lucia Dlugoszewski) would achieve this everythingness at this moment, and then with this work and mind side by side we would consider that exciting level of poetry in the space between us. Such a collaboration is, of course, a very arduous thing but really is the only premise that should admit collaboration at all.

In the costumes (Ralph Dorazio, designer) I do not want merely to achieve a painting or sculpture in motion (although I wish always a fresh new image full of beginning). It is the excitement of a visual image *touching* a human body. I don't want only the poetry of a garment or the poetry of a body. I want the poetry of the

9

costume-on-the-body. If red covers my shoulder, the magic is not red, but the human shoulder touching red, that should tingle every shoulder in the audience with a red tingle, not a blue tingle. If a branch is fastened across my face it is the drama between the branch and my face, and if a mask hides my face, it is the new absence of face that is the poetry.

In the choreography itself, far below the level of words, I would like to show the miracle of two people, the perfection of the one beside the perfection of the other and the poetry of the space between them. For the man and for the woman I would like to discover as many levels of movement as I, as a live person, can imagine from the gentlest opening of the mouth, the fastest blink of the eye, the tiniest wiggle of the toes, to the strangest leap and the deepest mystery of the spine.

Throughout the dance, for me, the delight would be to show the identity of man and woman, not their struggle for domination, not their aggressiveness toward each other. As a statement of my deep belief in woman, I would like to rescue man from his neuter, embarrassed role in the nineteenth and twentieth century ballet and give him a new image, almost unknown in our culture, where his strength would be not a necessary evil but a joy, where his physical liveness would be his deep refinement, where his beauty would be his gift of love.

The Western world is waiting for a new statement of the beautiful relationship between man and woman. Neither Christian nor Greek tradition gave many patterns of it. The troubadours' tradition still was incomplete. There are too few Walther von der Vogelweides. Only a few poets today speak to me of this: an e.e. cummings who can say, "one's not half two. It's two are halves of one," or perhaps a Paul Eluard when he speaks of what is good, of what helps him to live.

In Western art, movement has *never* achieved this. Almost the most beautiful myth comes from India in Shiva and Parvati. The two figures in my series of duets want to discover the way up to that essence. Neither the Kinsey report nor Margaret Mead can speak to the lonely bewildered allpeople the way the poetry of art can understand them, because a man and a woman together is poetry, and not scientific knowledge.

And what material of art, what clay is more rich than a hollow of the hand, the under armpit, the inside hungness of the knee. Jean Cocteau discovered a little of this in his *Blood of a Poet* when he visually grew a mouth in the palm of the hand. In the final duet I particularly want to search the whole body for the infinite possibilities of "The Tender Gesture." Biblically, in the beginning was the word; but now the tender gesture could resurrect the world.

(Of course, this is the difficult discipline, that successful, can change the death of a prophet into the life of a child; can make Paul Klee draw a picture; can make Charlie Chaplin say, "Simplicity is no simple thing.")

Three/ Modern Dance as a Voyage of Discovery

A lecture given at the San Francisco Museum of Art, June 1, 1959.

I

The most beautiful thing, the most exciting thing about modern dance is that nobody can define it. Yes, really, something has happened in America. Where at one time no one could possibly have spoken of the dance as an art in America, now one can and does and will.

No one can define modern dance. As soon as anyone can, it will be a dead one. But one can tell about it. I have to laugh up my sleeve when someone says, don't talk, just dance. Anybody worth his salt talks. When I am in love with someone, I always talk, don't you? Perhaps I can't define her, but I can certainly talk about her. I can tell about all the wondrous qualities of aliveness of her, and of her beauty, but of course never hit any final mark.

So now I cannot tell all about modern dance but I can tell what I feel about it. My feelings may change as I observe more, and dance more, but today these are my feelings. They are purely my feelings. They may be very strong feelings, very excited feelings, full of wonder, amazement, delight, and beauty.

So some of my feelings are about what I like, about what delights me, but also overlooked feelings about what is true. Certainly, we want to know what is true. So we must keep our eyes open. We had better see whether we are walking along a path that leads to a quicksand bog, or a camouflaged spiked pit.

Sometimes I find there is no alternative but to divide all individuals into two groups. I hate to do it, but it seems inevitable, really necessary. Some people seem to be curious. They look on everything in human nature and non-human nature with curiosity. The other group just isn't really curious about anything.

What I have to say about modern dance as a voyage of discovery will make sense only to those who are curious right down to the bottom of their boots. A voyage of discovery is not travel in a well-worn, well-known path. It's more like a direction somewhere. Modern dance is a direction, maybe several directions, ahead to somewhere we have never quite been before.

To be a discoverer generally means to be curious about something and to go toward it. Sometimes you get scared and think, "Good grief, where am I going?" Sometimes you might think if you're a discoverer, "God, no one's coming along after me." But a real discoverer keeps going on, to have the fun of discovering. Some people like to adventure and I am one of them.

There is a French term often used today in writing about art—*avant-garde*.[3] I guess it means that only the brave ones either are put or go up front. Anyway, when one reviewer in speaking about the first performance of my dance, "Here and Now With Watchers," at Hunter Playhouse a year ago, spoke of me as really and truly avant-garde, I was terribly pleased. If you're alive and kicking, what fun would there be in being anything else?

Next is to explain in some way my feelings about the direction or directions that modern dance is taking. The only way I know to talk about this is to recall what happens to me when I sit in the theatre, watching dancing.

It isn't in any way theoretical. It is about what happens to me when I sit and am a watcher. The delight that I feel then is the same delight I would like to make in the watchers who watch me dance and those who dance with me.

Maybe some of you have never thought of it before. What is dance? What is food? Have you ever had lunch or dinner with someone you were trying to impress, either to get a job or to interest in some way, or have you ever been anxious? We all have. Have you been fleetingly aware either then or later that you ate, but didn't really taste the food? Maybe if it was a special occasion you fleetingly knew it was especially good food, but you didn't taste it.

Have you ever been driving in the car way out in the mountains, beach or desert? Then, driving far from the road, you turned off the motor? Haven't we all had the sensation that the motor was making a noise that stopped, but we knew we hadn't heard it. Recollect now. Walking over here to the museum, do you remember the actual sensation of walking? You knew you walked. Probably you didn't know walking though, did you? Have you been in a concert hall and all at once known you hadn't heard, really heard, the sounds, though the musicians hadn't ceased to play?

It seems then, in the same way, that people can dance and people can watch people dance and still the dancers cannot feel they are dancing and the watchers not feel the dancing! In other words, dancing can be danced without the dancing being felt, experienced by the dancer or the watcher of the dance! There can be a kind of anaesthetic, a not-feeling!

When this is in the extreme, it is like prestidigitation. When something is done by sleight-of-hand by a magician, we know something has happened but we don't see it happen. We see a result. Now believe it or not, some dance tries to do this. It makes a result for the eye.

But my feeling is that the only dance that delights me is the exact opposite. It makes me aware of every infinitesimal moment of the movement, it shows me all the transitions of movement, it shows me the happening of the movement for its own sake, not for a result.

We are alive. We move and so can sense the movement of another living thing.

Whenever we see movement of a living creature we know this movement through what is called the kinesthetic sense. The word *kine* is a Greek root meaning movement. The "cinema" is moving things, movies. "Aesthetic" is a Greek root meaning feeling. "Anaesthetic" means not-feeling. "Kinesthetic" means feeling of movement.

The kinesthetic sense, the sensing of movement, is the heart of dance.

I have never found from a philosopher whether anyone else thinks of the kinesthetic sense as a sixth sense. But when you teach as many people every year as I do, you almost have to consider the kinesthetic sense as a sixth sense. Just as some people, unlike the sensitive Colette, are very inattentive in their noses and don't smell easily or completely, so it seems to me that people don't have a strongly developed kinesthetic sense. Movement is seen through the eye, isn't it, but the receptive organ is really not a differentiated organ, but the whole organ of the body's muscles and bones.

A few years ago, when my studio was over on Fifth Avenue (New

York), something happened that really showed me what I think is the primary material of dance, just as sound, any sound, is the primary material of music.

As I left the studio and was walking up the wide sidewalk, I was passing a bus stop and took in at a glance something very extraordinary and wondrous; very extraordinary because something happened to me before I could think about it or interpret it. I just felt.

A man afflicted badly with spastic paralysis was standing on the sidewalk at the bus stop. I saw him see the bus which he wanted to get on, coming rather fast. He could see it was not changing direction and realized he had to move out to it.

All this time, I was walking past and watching. It happened so fast, I couldn't have helped him. Because of his spastic paralysis, his legs were very unsymmetrical and as he walked, he threw his trunk far off balance, and his arms moved up convulsively.

In his anxiety he saw he had to get off the curb and out into the street to the bus. In stepping off-center, he had to make a distorted lurch.

As he did, I felt a terrible wrench in the horizontal center of my pelvis. It was as though the muscles were brought into action deep inside the pelvis, ones I had never been conscious of before.

My reaction showed me what I think is the heart of dance. From the first startling moments when by chance I saw [Harald] Kreutzberg and [Yvonne] Georgi,[4] I had fallen in love with sheer movement.

This experience, this immediate, direct feeling of my body watching the spastic-paralytic walk-fall off the curb, showed me that when we watch another person dance, we can feel his movement quite immediately in our own bodies.

This happening is an immediate apprehension through the seeing eyes into the spectator's own sense of body—muscles and bones—and the muscles moving the bones.

It is possible for you to imagine, to agree with me, that just as a color-blind person would not see different colors in a painting—degrees of grayness, yes, but not actual colors in their distinctions—so a spectator whose feeling for movement in his body was unawakened, unaware, would not see differences of movement of a person he was watching—he might not even "sense" the movement at all.

II

How does one learn to dance? A person could of course "teach" himself dance. All he would have to do is move himself. If he were to form the movement into a dance, into an art, then he would have to remember, sometimes analyze in order to remember, to arrange, to make distinctions—to compose the movement into a form of some kind.

But in no activity, generally, do we start from scratch individually and forfeit the experience of others, even in building a fire. No, we copy somebody. So in the process of learning the dance, we copy movements of someone until we have learned all the distinctions in movement they can show us.

How do we learn one movement from another? By watching. In my teaching, I find a very direct correlation between the student's personal technique of watching the world without daydreams (his imaginary film) and, therefore, of watching someone else's movement, and how he succeeds in doing the movement himself.

Learning dance happens directly through the kinesthetic sense. If this kinesthetic sense were well developed, no concepts, no theories, no words would ever need be used in the teaching and learning of dance. Each beginning student would learn simply by watching the movement of those who already could dance, and in time, when he was completely aware of himself, he would find his own individually felt movement and then if he wished, dance those discovered movements, put them into a form in his own dance.

In Tahiti, I have read, the Polynesians can talk to each other without making a sound. They move the eyes alone when they wish to. What they intend to convey to another is directly transmitted only through movements of the eye muscles.

When Sampih, the Balinese dancer, was in America, he came to my studio one day. Certainly as a joke mainly, since we couldn't speak much, he stood behind me and pretended to teach me Balinese movement by moving my arms with his outstretched hands. No books, no theories. Direct passage of feeling in the muscles.

I find that many students who come to study dance are quite

unaware of this possibility of kinesthetic (movement-feeling). They do not know how to watch and then sense in their own bodies and do the movements themselves directly and simply. They wait for a concept about movement to be put into words. Instead of watching me flex (that is, bend) the ankle, for example, and doing so themselves, they wait for me to say, "Flex the ankle." Then you would be surprised how sometimes the feeling for their own body movement is so atrophied that even when watching and hearing me say the words, nothing happens muscularly in their bodies.

While I have been speaking just now of dance in the learning process, I am interested in leading you to see what happens in the theatre in the art of dance.

The first material, first ingredient, first possibility, of dance as an art, of dance as a performance is just this. Before anything else happens, the very essence of dance is that the spectator watch the actual movement of the bones of the dancer in space.

You do recognize, I am sure, that no movement occurs unless bones are moved in space by muscles. Oh, I guess the blink of eyelids or rolling of eyes occurs without bone movement, or when a horse twitches his flanks to scare off the flies. But otherwise, an act of muscles has to move bones of the skeleton in space for us to speak of body movement.

The spectator sees the movement of the dancer and translates it directly into his own body sensation. When it happens, and it doesn't automatically happen, no, not at all, this is the first thing that happens.

It is the heart of dance.

Everyone takes for granted that this happens all the time when someone watches a dancer. But it really doesn't.

The main revolution in what was called modern dance was based on this observation, this knowledge, and how exciting it is, how very exciting it is. But knowing about it has been forgotten or obscured. I will go into that later. The revolution in our art of dance, still to be made, is to face this fact squarely, look at it, get excited all over again, and explore it.

But you can see it is a two-way art. The dancer has to move in such a way to make this very visible, very conscious, and the watchers have to be able to see it and let—remember the word, let—it happen to them.

You can't have cotton in your ears when you expect to hear the sounds music is made up of, and you can't have cotton in your body when you watch dance.

III

I think I have explained enough, intimated enough, suggested for your own experience-memory enough about kinesthesis, about the kinesthetic sense, about the primary element of the art of dance, to introduce some of you now to the statement of a philosopher, without which all talk about dance or any other art is, in my opinion, ring around the rosey.

The reason this philosopher's statement about art is so illuminating, so exciting, is that it is not out on a limb by itself but is right at the root and trunk together with science and philosophy. His statement about art is part and parcel of everything man knows about anything, anywhere in the world, at any time. The ideas I shall try to give you, a brief indication as they relate to art, do not contradict any aspects of science, philosophy or religion for they are all part of one single investigation of how man knows.

This philosopher, who is a scientist too, in his investigation of science, because he is a sensitive thinker, had to, he couldn't help it, investigate art.

He found that one must speak of two functions of art, two ways art works. You might call them two ends of a pole. Any work of art could be located at any small division point located anywhere along the pole between its two ends. So you see, any point on the pole would be closer to one end or the other of the pole, and so be farthest away from the opposite end of the pole. In between, you then see, there is only relative closeness to either absolute end. That is a pretty good analogy with which to speak of any given work of art.

This philosopher calls the two poles the first function of art and the second function of art. The first function of art is when art deals only in the primary elements of all arts—the senses. It is awareness! Through the senses we immediately apprehend colors, shapes, sounds, smells and textures, for example. These are the primary materials of art. They are ineffable. That means there is nothing to say about them. You either see the color blue or you don't. You hear a sound or you don't. You either smell coffee being made or you don't.

What is the second function of art then? It is this. These sights, sounds, smells, textures and tastes can be used to "say something" about ideas. If I crooked my index finger this way and wiggled it back and forth towards me, what would you see? Say I did that movement in a dance. Would you call it a movement in the first or second function of art? I guess everybody would say I was using the wiggling of the finger in order to beckon you to come to me. You can see that is second function. If I could wiggle that finger and all you saw was the actual movement of the finger, done for no meaning, no purpose, with no association of any kind, then we could speak of the movement as art in the first function—the art of awareness of awareness.

I have tried the following little trick on a number of students. Say I painted the upper horizontal half of a rectangular white wall panel with a nice light blue. When I ask what do you see, some people always, without hesitation, say blue and some people always say sky.

You can see that those who say blue are seeing the color in its first function, a color immediately apprehended, ineffable. It is there for its own sake.

But then you see that those who said sky have seen the blue, not in itself for its own sake, but as a means of conveying information about something other than itself.

Isn't this way of thinking about art exciting! You would have to read the philosopher's whole book to understand all the implications, to understand that these two complementary ways of discriminating the two functions of art are also analogous to the two main ways of knowing the world.

This insight was come upon by a philosopher named F.S.C. Northrop. His statement about art is the most fundamental in the history of Western thought. He presents this in his book, *The Meeting of East and West.*

IV

You will remember that earlier I spoke of the kinesthetic sense, the sense whereby you feel movement. Now you can make a sound with your own voice and hear it, or you can hear the sound I make with my voice. In the same way you can wiggle your toes and "sense" that you are doing it. Or you can see a dancer wiggle his toes and feel it because you know what it feels like in your own toes.

So you can see better now what the kinesthetic sense implies. It is the primary basis of either dancing yourself or watching someone else. When a dancer does a dance movement purely for itself, for its own sake, and for someone to watch purely for its own sake, there you see we have dance as an art in its first function. It is the first miracle—awareness of awareness!

When a dancer does a movement and uses the movement to convey some idea to us, he uses movement as a means, not for itself. What the movement feels like doesn't matter. It is not done for its own sake. That is why in art in its first function, one person can't tell another what it is. One either sees it or one doesn't. With art in its second function, one can more easily find some words to tell another person what it is meant to convey. Only art in its second function is art as language!

So now we have come to a place where I might talk about a word that has been the main stumbling block in the revolution called modern art. The large mass of the public (in this democratic culture where everyone is equal, yet obviously "unequal") trips and stumbles on the word "understand" when trying to respond to any modern art. "I don't understand it."

Now there are other aspects of the problem, but you have jumped the gun, I'm sure, and have seen for yourself that when art is veering mainly toward the first function, there is *nothing to* understand. I don't *understand* the smell of coffee. I just smell it or, if I have a cold, I don't smell it. Of course, sometimes when I smell the coffee, when I have just opened my eyes, I do understand that breakfast is ready. Oh, luxury!

So one can't understand the materials of any art in their primary function. One can only perceive them. This is miraculous. The first time I intellectually got this was when I read that Picasso said, "Why try to understand the language of birds?" I think I must say once more that art in the second function is conveyed by means of the first function. Later, we shall see that this is a very important point in considering dance as an art.

When we first performed "Here and Now With Watchers" (1957), some spectators said to me later, "It was beautiful, but I didn't understand it."

One day in rehearsal, I was thinking about the dance and the music and the costumes, and realized that we had tried to make an adventure in totality in the primary function of art. However, the "clown" and the final duet, "like DARLING," veered toward the second function. So, in general, you see, the movements, sounds, colors, shapes, were just to be perceived through the senses. For the most part, there was nothing to understand. No language. I believe this will clear up now some of our thinking about art and dance. Both primary and secondary functions of all arts are there, inevitably to be used, and always have been. They are complementary polarities of direction. They are analogous to the two ways of knowing the world—the one, immediate apprehension; the other, through the theoretical, as in science. It takes both to complete our knowledge of the world. Science itself uses both, as does art.

Since the way of the West has been primarily the way of science, up until the revolution which created "modern art,"[5] the emphasis in our Western art has been on the second function of art. Art was used as a means to convey ideas known through science, philosophy, and religion. The modern revolution was the recognition that art in and for itself, that is, art in its first function, was also good, complete, and of equal importance. It was really the pure fact of existence.

But different arts have traveled in the revolution at different speeds.

I believe that many people feel that the revolution in modern art has been completed. But I really think—it is my surest conviction—that we are still in the middle of the revolution. I use the word revolution here meaning that the attempt is not to overturn anything, but to fill in a partial concept of art and discover a *total* one.

The voyage of discovery in the primary function of art, or movement in and for itself, in the magical pure fact of existence, is still awaiting those dancers who will make that trip.

A while ago, I took time to try to see with you what the basis of dance really was. I tried to convey to you how the kinesthetic sense is the basis of dance, as sound is the basis of music.

May I say again that human beings can move in their bodies and not know they are moving. In the same way, I have shown you that dancers can dance and watchers can watch and not really experience the actual moment-by-moment movement. Have you ever made some action that involved quite a bit of movement in the body and later realized you did it without being aware of it at the time. Strange as it may seem, I think this happens in dance. However, all the exciting dance I have ever seen from all over is when that does *not* happen.

Putting dance back into the body as a moment-by-moment sensation is part of the voyage, is part of the revolution.

V

I cannot at this time go into why in the West the dance has left the moment-by-moment sensation of movement of muscles and bones. But it has. It certainly and definitely has. Of course, not with everybody. We are all human beings and can, if we don't hinder ourselves, partake of what every human being can experience. But in the West in general—from the Jewish prudery put forth in the basic myth of the Garden of Eden, up through Plato, who identified the aesthetic way of knowing the world with the body, with the female principle and then with evil, up through Catholicism and Protestantism—we have considered the body as impermanent, untrustworthy, as a way to know reality, and, therefore, dirty. So we in the West have danced, but our underlying feeling has been to do it in spite of ourselves, just as we look on our sexual life as a necessary evil, in other words, because we are human. In this way, we have always been at war with ourselves. This was one of my earliest and most poignant intuitions as I grew up. It led me to do the dance, "Stephen Acrobat" (1947).

So does it not seem clear, do you not intuit what I say, way back in the feeling of your bones, that we in the West have always really considered the body dirty. A few honest souls, of course, have lived their lives as full human beings and lived in their bodies quite completely, but all authorities, all religions, all philosophies in the West have said, "Don't. Don't live in or love your bodies." We have separated nature and man, and the body is, of course, nature in man.

VI

One of the aspects of the voyage, then, will be living in the body moment-by-moment. To find the balance, we shall have to give attention to this in our technique, in our dance, for some time. You will all remember that Isadora Duncan started this revolution in Western dance. She said take off the shoes, feel the remarkable, wondrous human foot. Take off the corsets, tight bodices, feel the alive human spine. But as you know, people can take off externals and still not feel deeply in muscles and bones.

In this way, it seems that while we have made quite a change of attitude, the full way will come really only with a change of philosophy. Only through this philosophic change of attitude in looking at what we human beings are, will we arrive at our full possibility. There is no duty in this. It is only that each one of us, if he has the imagination, can experience his life to the fullest.

I believe it may be largely here that the qualitative leap onto another plateau of human experience in the West is possible. I tread on thorny ground when I try to analyze these questions and make a comparison with traditional ballet as it is taught and created today. I expect to convince no one by anything I might say. I am not an evangelist. I say merely look and see whether what I say may be true. Each one of us is such a complex of often unrelated ideas that reason or argument itself is of no value. It seems there is a faculty in us called "intellectual intuition." Each one of us has to recognize for himself whether some observation holds water. Often, this takes time.

The plain democratic majority of custom and interest is against what I have to say. The real vested interests, the desire for wider performances, easier jobs, faster agreement in working ideas, are contrary to what I think I have observed as so.

May I say it this way. The reason we as spectators, sitting in the seats, or we as dancers, composing and dancing new dances, need the revolution, the direction called "modern dance," and the reason why it is inevitable, is because the tradition of dance which grew up in the Renaissance in Europe, which we now call ballet, is "theoretical." It is based on a concept of movement of the human body which is essentially diagrammatic and opposed to the immediately apprehended kinesthetic sense of movement.

But don't misunderstand me. Have you ever seen the Chinese symbol of the world as two polarities? These polarities are the yin and yang. They are represented by a black and white area, each like a comma, which fitting together, are enclosed in a circle. The Chinese signify all the polarities of the world into this symbol, but in the center of the black and white commas is a small dot of the opposite.

We must take what I am saying in this way. Due to the scientific ideas (the theoretical way of knowing the world) which occupied the West so completely from the Renaissance on, due to the philosophic ideas which stemmed from and reacted with the scientific ideas of the time, the overall feeling about the human body has to follow this lead. One of the most exciting ideas which we need to recognize and deal with today is that art is not in a vacuum. It, of necessity, has to proceed from scientific and philosophic ideas.

You have perhaps observed the insignia or trademark used from its inception by the School of American Ballet founded under George Balanchine's leadership. It is a man's figure with arms and legs spread out in such proportions to reach an enclosed circle. It is obvious that it has the intention of showing the human figure in an analytical and theoretical aspect.

It is actually a Renaissance concept analogous to the interest of the time in dissecting human corpses. It is an expression of the theoretical interest in the body. It is essentially allied with a scientific way of knowing the human body.

This way of knowing the body is opposite to the way the body is sensed through immediate apprehension, through direct experiencing. This is a large subject and I cannot go into it further here. But as I speak later of some very pressing questions about the relation of ballet and modern dance, I shall return to this general statement.

A very clear analogy to the underlying philosophic basis of ballet is the painting of the Renaissance. You will all recognize that the chief goal of painting of the Renaissance until the revolution called modern painting was the development of scientific optics. As you recall, the invention of the photograph in one sweep said, "Don't bother with that old kind of painting at all." And so we don't today. Oh, of course, there is the National Academy of Design, but who pays attention to it? Imitation antiques!

So in painting we have a whole new world—what a renaissance of painting in the Western world today! The change came from a philosophic development of attention to the primary function of art.

Isadora Duncan was the harbinger of the inevitable change in the art of dance due to the change of philosophic thought. I never saw Isadora, of course. She was dead long before I ever knew there was such a thing as dance as an art. She took only baby steps in reaching toward a new possibility in dance. The only place in the history of Western culture where she saw the body as a possible instrument of art was classical Greece, so she couldn't help being fed by its images.

But she did definitely change the current in the West by putting the feeling, the kinesthetic feeling, into the body. For this we can always love and honor her. If you compare a photograph of hers, which would exemplify what I am talking about, and one of Pavlova or Nijinsky—if you are aware of what I am talking about at all—I am sure you will intuit the difference. Of course, it might seem that the kinesthetic sense-awareness might not be observable in a photograph, but unless I am imagining it, it is. I can merely report what I sense when I look.

Isadora's writings are still thrilling to me. Read her collected essays in *The Art of the Dance*. Many aesthetic problems in creating a dance art that are true to today, she didn't face at all.

She couldn't have. She did enough anyway. Her use of "great" classical music for dance was taken up by the ballet and modern dance. Maybe she had no alternative; we were so green and the revolution in music was so slow. It is as slow as that in dance. Her advocation of the "great masters" is still polluting our own dance art even in so-called modern dance.

But she did see that the whole philosophic premise of ballet was outmoded and inadequate and she saw that it had to be superseded. I am amazed at the pigeon-holing in the minds of those who today pay lip service to her but espouse principles of dance contradictory to her main premise, and do not see that we have to recognize constantly what is and then proceed from there to build our art.

Every condemnation Isadora made of the ballet in 1900 through 1920 is still true today as I see it.

But in the 1920s, the revolution was continued by others and so modern dance in America existed. The history of this I cannot go into here. It is too exciting not to go into deeply and I hope to another time. All I wish to say is that I believe that all expressions of how we approach and create art inevitably follow from the total scientific and philosophic ideas of the time—the ideas of the good. With Einstein's work in 1904, the Western world, indeed all the world, changed. Modern dance as a direction in art was a very necessary consequence. Isadora's existence in 1904 was part of it. Modern dance had to be born. Once the vision of it existed, ballet was doomed, doomed to extinction.

It is dead. It is simply that most people, of course, do not know it. Even the modern dancers who are "modern dancers" by circumstance, rather than knowledge, don't completely sense it is doomed.

It may hang on an unconscionably long time, I am sorry to say. For there is a great lag.

I can tell you a personal story to illustrate. When I was a boy of fifteen at Harvard, a professor in a class reading of *The Birds* in Greek, told us that Harvard was building all the first seven houses of its new house plan in a blown-up Colonial style. It was a major building time in Harvard's history.

I honor still Professor Post's insight. He said then that if the authorities of Harvard had known it, there had been the opportunity to create a totally new contemporary style for America, one that would be us.

The sequel is that when the plans are published this year for the eighth house—all these years later—it is a contemporary architecture—architecture as modern art. But such could have been created at the beginning. Poor Harvard was not alone.

Do you know what eclecticism is? At that time, Yale, in her great expansion, built Gothic architecture. Yet right in those years the philosopher Alfred Whitehead at Harvard, whom I used to see as an old man walking along the Charles River was writing: "The most unGreek-like thing one can do is to copy the Greeks." Yes, the ballet may be with us a while yet.

I think I can give you another personal experience of how untrue to ourselves we can be. When I was first journeying east from Kansas City to see the world, I went to Washington and to the Lincoln Memorial.

As I went inside and looked up at the large sculpture, I was moved by Lincoln's words carved into the walls, and when I walked among the columns, I was deeply moved. I sensed the beautiful proportions of the building, its scale, its simplicity, its clarity.

Do you know the word "pastiche"? The dictionary says: *pastiche*—a patchwork, a medley, a work of art imitating a previous work, a work of art made up of various sources. The word implies making something new to look as though it had been made at some previous period.

We all know in our hearts and our intelligence that the Lincoln Memorial is a pastiche, a bankrupt expression in architecture of honor to an original man like Lincoln.

I think you can now sense that I conceive of modern dance as a direction of the human spirit here in America in the making of art which cannot repeat, relive, rewarm, stand still, copy or revert or keep corpses alive.

VII

Has it ever struck you that ballet technique in the late eighteenth and nineteenth centuries was paralleling the Industrial Revolution? You do see, don't you, that the Industrial Revolution resulted from the theoretical, scientific philosophy starting with the Renaissance. Theoretical knowledge allowed the invention of machines. Men were entranced by machines.

You do recognize that the toe shoe, by the second half of the nineteenth century, was a machine. It used the human foot not for its own sake in the immediacy of its feeling, but immobilized it to attain *quantity*, as in turning. The more revolutions a wheel in a machine could attain, the more turns a dancer could make. It was treated as a national holiday when the first native-born Russian woman dancer in the czar's Imperial School learned to complete thirty-two perfect fouettés. Fouettés you have all seen—a whip of a leg spins the dancer a whole turn on the pointe of the standing leg.

You may think it funny but it really isn't. This imitation of the machine made people do all kinds of mechanical ballets. Mechanical dolls, ballets méchaniques, and finally, the Rockettes. When fifty girls high kick in unison, like something in a great spinning machine or printing press, the audience is delighted and claps. We are the machine. Or think we are.

You maybe have never heard of the word "coenesthesia." The dictionary says: the undifferentiated complex of organic sensation forming the essence of our sense of body and bodily condition.

So now maybe you can recognize that the total body feeling, the total coenesthesia, of the person trained in ballet technique goes in the direction of the theoretical, and ultimately, the mechanical. One night, a couple of years ago, as I was going to sleep after reflecting on a performance of ballet at the City Center, I sat up in bed and said to myself, "Yes, the ballet technique in essence is the brain driving the body."

This direction in coenesthesia is an error and fails to know, really sense, what we are.

We are animals.

Wonderful two-legged animals.

Plus.

We have the same seven neck vertebrae as the giraffe and the dolphin. We have the same pelvis, thigh sockets, hearts, genitals as the other animals with our kind of vertebrae, the vertebrates. Our muscles and nerves organize the same way.

The difference between men and animals is a big philosophical subject. But I do know we have a common structure, a common necessity to move as the animals do. The only statement about our existence that cannot be contradicted by anyone is that our existence depends on our moving our muscles.

That is our existence.

That, we have in common with all the animals. The beautiful animals.

It is true I choose among the animals as to their movement. I do choose. I choose the tiger and the leopard, the snake, the fish, the peacock, the prancing horse.

In the West, we have felt we were above nature, that we had to conquer nature. So we developed the electric light to conquer night and the airplane to conquer air.

As we arrive in the West to a less one-sided understanding of our life, I think we will sense how to cooperate with nature. In ballet technique, the attempt is essentially to dominate nature. Of course, it is fun to jump. All humans jump. But in ballet technique, the jump is to conquer, to *conquer* gravity.

I submit there is another way, a way I find more beautiful. To feel in the body. That is, to cooperate with nature. To feel gravity.

To yield, rest in it, play with it, sense instant-by-instant the unfathomable complexity of relationships of the weight of the body as dance happens. All the dance that has made my hair stand on end and made me cry out "Beautiful!" has done this whether at one end of the earth or the other—all the way from the Watusis to the Hopis.

I am sure you see that how we dance stems from our total philosophic view of our human life and, insofar as our philosophic idea is partial or has gaps in it, our dance can be stiffened or set, become limited or only partially functioning. You see that the challenge to the human race is always to see *what is*. That is the challenge to our dance today—to question all basic premises and partial intuitions so that we don't limit ourselves in our own exploration of our human possibilities, until the day we die.

The tendency to experience our life only through the partial, theoretical way was so common in recent Western thinking that it was poked fun at by Charles Dickens in a wonderful book, *Hard Times*. A little girl whose father ran a small traveling family circus made up mainly of horses and a wonderful performing dog named Merrylegs was sent, while the family was in a small town in England, to the local school.

The school teacher, whose principle of teaching was "We want nothing but Facts! Stick to the Facts, sir," calls on her. "Give me your definition of a horse."

She is thrown into the greatest alarm by this.

"Girl number Twenty unable to define a horse! Bitzer, your definition of a horse."

"Quadruped, graminivorous. Forty teeth, namely twenty-four grinders, four eye-teeth, and twelve incisive. Sheds coat in spring—" and so on.

The little girl, Sissy, has been brought up with horses all her life. She knows the horse nature, the living experience, but of course, couldn't define a horse.

I feel that in the subtlest ways imaginable the theoretical way of knowing movement has been the predominant way of dance in its theatre form called ballet since the Renaissance, until Isadora Duncan caught a glimpse of another possibility.

I believe that anyone who has been very observant will have

noticed that balletic coenesthesia is almost completely—I say almost completely—diagrammatic.

As the well-trained balletic dancer studies and moves, the inner sense of what the movement should look like is essentially the clarity of a geometrical design. Observe any book illustrating ballet and I think you will see what I mean. Its premise is a theoretical one. The movement is felt as a static geometrical relationship of vertical trunk with arms and legs moving like semaphores. Now this doesn't always happen. The unconscious human feeling and sense spills out. But the avowed technique aims at a machine-like sense of symmetry.

I believe my real intuition was confirmed when by accident a few years ago, I saw both the Eastern and Western treatment of a swan in dance.

Swanness.

An attempt, that is, to find in movement on the stage the poetry of the swan.

A dancer—an extraordinary dancer named Priyagopal—came to America from a little-known section of northeast India called Manipur. It has a long, rich dance tradition, and Priyagopal was of a long line of dancers-musicians. One time in New York, he gave a study in silence, without costume, of a heron and later one of a swan. Afterwards, he spoke in his good, but hesitant, English about how he felt about watching the swan, even how the swan ate.

This short piece was a masterpiece of poetic insight. Sensitive, observant, subtle, egoless, at one with the wondrousness of the living swan, the living world.

About the same time, I saw a much-praised performance of the ballet "Swan Lake" at the Metropolitan Opera House. Of course, I had seen it often before, but coming just after Priyagopal's performance, I was shocked to see the absence of inner awareness, the dull coenesthesia of the movement of the "swan" in the ballet. The movement was inorganic and, I have to use the word, theoretical. I am not at all talking about body experience, body sense, body feeling. The movements were broken, jerky, unflowing.

Then consider the design of the choreography. Do you recall the straight lines, the symmetrical groupings, the unsubtle walkings? Of course, the final absurdity is the dance of the four cygnets.

Can you imagine any four dancers behaving more like a machine?

Even when they stop the dance, the effect is like pulling the switch of a machine.

The underlying feeling of balletic technique is in an opposite direction to sensing the beauty of cooperation with nature—with the nature in us, the nature we are, and are a part of, rather than trying to dominate nature.

VIII

Up to this point, I have been talking about the first function of art. In dance, this is movement of the human body and I have been trying to see whether we were missing the beat. Ballet, as it is taught in principle, *is,* in my opinion. Let me cease to use for the moment the abstraction, modern dance.

Let us face it.

The modern dance is the "modern dancers," just as modern painting is the modern painters. And while they are aiming in a general direction—at least not trying to stand still—inwardly they may be proceeding with principles at variance with each other.

Nothing wrong with that, for them. But it is for us to look at what is happening and evaluate it as we can or may or will.

Everything I have said up to now will, I hope, elucidate my point of view—this very important question. One of the most immediate questions which confronts any young student who says he wishes to be a modern dancer is this: Some people who say they believe in the modern dance advise me to study ballet. Shall I?

No answer comes to my mind that answers this better than Jesus' advice! "Don't put new wine into old goat skin bags for the old bags, now dry, static, ready to split, will split and you'll lose your wine. Put your new wine into new goat skin bottles."

Now technique is no absolute. Technique in dance is a means of being ready in dance, to perform the movements in the theatre that you will want to use in your dance. If you want to perform the work of art called "Swan Lake," for example, study the technique that will prepare you for doing so.

If you want to learn to shuffle cards with your toes as Bondini did, then studying the technique that will enable you to dance one of the little swans in "Swan Lake" won't help you. May I ask: Is modern dance a full-fledged art or is it not? Is it saying and being something new or is it not? If it is, then I think it will have its own technique, complete and sufficient for what it wishes to be in the theatre. If it doesn't have its own technique, then what is it, and how does it even exist? If it doesn't exist, then what is everybody talking about?

I think we may safely say it exists. I have seen the performances of masterpieces called modern dance and, I think, have danced in some of them.

I say this: If any artist creating in modern dance feels a necessity to study ballet, then I say he or she has not worked hard enough in his own art. If in his own art, his own aesthetic, he wishes to prepare the body to move in certain areas, then let him work on those technical exercises like any human being who wants to dance. Turnout of the legs doesn't belong to ballet. Complete action of the foot, both to point and to flex, doesn't belong to ballet technique. Hindu dance, among others, has achieved it more completely.

The artist can use any movement he wishes, and therefore train his body to execute it, if he will just work hard enough in his own studio and work hard enough with training his own pupils. The technique in modern dance if it is to be worth its salt will include the widest range of movement it is interested in. Please consider the words "interested in." For this is the essence of the problem.

If you are bored with certain movements which have by now been performed in every ballet *ad nauseam*, if you are interested in new works of art and wouldn't be caught dead doing worn-out movements, why spend your time practicing them in an old framework? Find your new framework right in your own studio. I consider it an admission of bankruptcy and laziness for an artist in modern dance to advocate ballet training.

IX

Now I need to recall to you all I said earlier about how the body can be sensed.

All of the theoretical and technical principles of ballet lead to one kind of coenesthesia. In my opinion, this does not result in the most beautiful movement true to the human body or make it ready to create poetry on stage. No, the beautiful movement I have seen in modern dance, when it was true to itself, when it had entered the revolution or the beautiful movement of all other peoples, was outside the balletic tradition of Europe. Often people ask me to try to put into a few words the technical difference between ballet and modern dance.

I have talked about the first underlying difference—how the body feels as it has been awakened to feel in the most completely sensed way, true to its own nature and possibility.

I may mention, however, two other general ideas that are actually a subdivision of the underlying coenesthesia.

Part of the theoretical aspect of balletic movement is that it was thought that registerable positions—arabesques, attitudes, jumps—are made to the fullest extent of the body. Of course, movement moves. But all you have to do to understand what I mean is to watch different people walk. Some walk aware of their weight and relation to gravity—that is, walking is falling. So the movement passes on. It transits—goes through moment-by-moment. Others, at the opposite end of the scale, walk brokenly without passage or shift of weight and without the greatest economy.

Modern dance, when understood by the dancer in this point in its early revolution, tried to explore the transition of movement—tried to make the movement move most completely.

The other subdivision also comes from the theoretical premise of ballet since the Renaissance. Ballet technique, in its principle, emphasizes a vertical trunk and allows the arms and legs to move separately. Watch a woman ballet dancer draw one leg up the side of the other and extend it out, which is called a développé, and you will see the separateness of leg and trunk. Of course the leg is connected to the trunk. All dancers are human, but so is a sculptor who carves a lace ruff in stone.

So this subdivision of coenesthesia which motivated the early exploration of movement in modern dance, starting with Isadora, is the awareness that the trunk initiates all movement and the arms, legs and head are tassels to the movement of the pelvis and spine.

When this is understood by a modern dancer, then he knows that to study ballet is to espouse an entirely contradictory action-feeling of how human movement occurs with the greatest ease, power, beauty, and possibility of wide expressiveness, in other words, poetry.

Modern dance has to exist. It is a larger principle than ballet. It is an attempt to discover a more comprehensive and total way of knowing Western movement and aesthetic in dance. The freely inquiring human mind inevitably has to keep sensing the larger principle to include more of our human experience. It is no accident, no, not at all, that modern dance in the Western world really started and developed in the United States.

People in ballet often act as though "modern dance" is a freak. As though it were the half-baked crazy art of some talented and some untalented off-beat odd ones who might have hit on something to contribute to the "mainstream" of dancing, "the ballet," or at least some gimmick good enough to steal from. But the truth is the other way around. Modern dance is the larger principle.

Just as modern poetry replaced Victorian and Georgian poetry, so too has modern dance superseded ballet.

Just as when modern painters and sculptors explored nonrepresentational subjects, the academic painting and academic sculpture aesthetic disappeared as a living principle in the eyes of those who care about the deepest excitement in art, so a similar event occurred in the art of dance.

Just as modern architecture replaced the eclectic "Beaux Arts" architecture of the nineteenth and early twentieth century, so too did modern dance replace the partial principle of movement and aesthetic of European and European-transplanted-into-American ballet.

X

Up to this point we have been speaking almost entirely of the dancer's movement itself, the pure fact of human movement in all its possibility of sheer beauty. Movement in all its living mystery is the principal material in the art of dance in its first function, just as colors and shapes are in painting, or sounds are in music.

The second function of art is in the use of this wondrous primary material, movement, to convey extra ideas or aspects of human experience or knowledge other than the movement in and for its own sake.

When a young boy jumps up and grabs a stationary trapeze bar and works up a momentum so that he swings back and forth, this is movement in its first function. But if by that swinging, he intended to convey to us that all human life swings back and forth between sorrow and happiness, between good and evil, between man and woman, between life and death, he would be using the movement to convey ideas not directly pertaining to the movement, or movement in its second function. Remember the possibility I spoke of earlier of looking at a patch of blue paint and seeing blue or seeing sky.

Modern dance as a potential will be a voyage of discovery in our Western world in the second function of art as well as in the first.

When in a dance the choreographer uses dance in its second function, then he takes on a great responsibility. If the ideas he tries to convey are infantile, adolescent, or senile, please deliver me from the boredom. If they are untrue to human experience, don't infect me with errors and set up a pattern of behavior before me that is neurotic unless you transform them with the insight of true tragedy. If they are paltry, then I ask for more from art.

The challenge of dance as an art today is that in its second function it should and can grow up to be a mature art, like the other arts. It would be here that one would have to make distinctions. Do you want entertainment, light classics, show business, or art? You can't have all or any combination at the same time. They are "saying" different things about human experience.

I take it we would all agree that when we speak of modern dance we mean dance as a modern art. Do not imagine that today art in America will have a wide audience. We are not an artistic nation. Only five percent of the people of America buy one book a year, I am told, so do not be afraid, modern dancers, that you have no wide audience, and imagine that you have failed. Mature your art and see what an intensive, alive expression you can find.

In the second function of art as well, modern dance has a very long voyage of exploration ahead. When I go to the theater I want to see dance in the second function capable of handling the most mature statements on our human experience such as I find in many beautiful modern works of art.

When I see a Modigliani painting of a woman's body lying on a bed in her beautiful nakedness, I am moved and see its truth. So when I see a dance, I want to see that woman portrayed in the dance not as a domineering combination of a czar's mistress, acrobat, and coquette, but as we can know and feel our experience of a woman in an e.e. cummings poem today or in our own experience—her, her fullness of nobility as a woman.

May I elaborate here a little further? When an art enters into the second function, its means and material in the first function must be rich enough to convey the complete essence of the second function aspect. One can't paint the subject of Picasso's "Guernica" with the technique of a sign painter, nor in a theatre collaboration, use the poems of Rimbaud with the first function movement of a musical comedy.

So the modern dance has advanced, can, and I believe, will and must advance on the level of both first and second functions. Personally, I believe the greatest challenge at the present time lies in discovery and building our new dance in the actual movement material. We have only just rediscovered it! But dance, of course, like all other arts, will constantly slide along the scale between the two poles or one might say, the two ends of the same pole of art in its first function and art in its second function.

Let me emphasize, again, that art to be valid must always in its second function interpret the most recent and correct scientific and philosophical ideas of the time. The artist, using the second function, does not originate the ideas he expresses. They can never contravene the most complete philosophic insights of the time of their expression by the artist. For example, we could not today make a dance which said, "The sun goes around the earth." Nor, except at our peril, can we express falseness about the relationship between men and women, or reinterpret myths, to distort their mysterious truth.

In such a way too, a dancer/choreographer must know the aesthetics of other arts—of all the arts of his time and of the philosophical ideas of his time. Otherwise he falls into the pit.

For example, suppose a choreographer says he is going to make a dance—a new work of art.

It is clear to us, is it not, that for the work of art to be valid, the dancer must convey the aesthetic ideas of his own time. I feel that if he is going to make a new work of art, a dance, it will not be new if he copies old movement such as courtly bows and puts this in his dance. We all know, don't we, that we don't behave or feel that way. So a falseness enters. In the same way, in a new work of art, we don't go to the museum of costume art and borrow great-grandfather's clothes to costume the dance. That would be ridiculous in a new work of art. In a similar way, in a new dance, a new work of art, we cannot borrow the music of our ancestors. That is too easy!

It has always been easy to eat today's meat and today's potatoes, but look at and hear yesterday's art. And it is wonderful to look at yesterday's art, but it is death to make yesterday's art today.

We always have to live in our own skins. Each man and woman always has to experience his or her own life. No father can go out from the safe village and encounter the monsters and kill them for us. We have to do it ourselves.

So, too, in art. As artists in the modern dance, we have to go on a voyage of discovery constantly. There is no other way if we are to live. This discovery, this revolution which is still to be made in dance, is in that pure fact of existence, that awareness of awareness, that first function of art—the material of dance itself for its own sake in transition before your eyes, instant-by-instant, before it is meanings, associations, or language—the immediately apprehended and eternal "now."

To find this, we dancers shall constantly have to keep asking the new questions.

As audiences too, we create the works of art today through asking.

To ask is to evoke the right response.

Four/ Questions and Answers

This essay, dated January 4, 1962, was written in response to questions posed by the editor of the Wagner College magazine.

Why do you dance barefoot?

What attracted Guiscart's attention most in Ramie was her feet. To Guiscart's mind came the puny, corn-deformed, ill-treated feet of Parisian girl models, the flesh inflamed where their shoes pressed hard. He thought too of the coarse, in-variably foul-odored deformity-ridden feet of the male models.

He could not take his eyes off Ramie's. They were absolute in their perfection. He often said that just as nine tenths of the people in the modern world never noticed the intelligence of a face, so is all sense of the beauty of the human foot lost to them.

Henri Montherlant in "La Rose du Sable"

What do you consider the most beautiful dance?

Dance that is violent clarity.
Dance that is effortless.
Dance that can at all times reveal a tender breastbone.
Dance that lets itself happen.
Dance that dedicatedly loves the pure fact of movement.
Dance that knows the most beautiful and true movement starts in the pelvis and spine and flows into the tassel-like legs, arms, and head.
Dance that uses technique that is an organic whole, not a grab bag of eclecticism.
Dance that does not stay in the mind, even the avant-garde mind.
Dance that senses itself instant-by-instant like the prick of a pin.
Dance that is aware of the music instant-by-instant.
Dance that loves gravity rather than fights gravity.
Dance that hangs and falls rather than fights.
Dance that has reached such a height of subtlety it can stand still.

Dance that loves time, time as a sensed duration, and all the subtle asymmetrical divisions of time, and yet always the pulse of time.

Dance that never ignores, either audience, or music or stage, or fellow dancers. Therefore, no frozen faces.

Dance that does not try to explode the same bubble twice. Neo-Dadaism being exactly that: the already exploded bubble.

Dance that is not a sheer shambles and general mess, a new Dada, anything goes, throw it together, kid stuff.

Dance that is grown-up, composed by post-adolescents for post-adolescents.

Dance that knows soundness in psyche and body always produces rhythmical movement; that spastic and catatonic-like movement is illness.

Dance that knows movement and music put together without a common pulse is two people talking at you at the same time. Something is ignored!

Dance that knows you must have live musicians as well as live dancers or you have dead music and dead theatre.

Dance that knows the longer records are used, the longer it will take us to find the correct music for dance.

Dance that is aware of what a woman is and what a man is.

Dance that knows how to show that the love of man and woman is neither soupy nor misery.

Dance that reveals the dance and the dancer.

Dance that knows that the art is more than the personality of the dancer.

Dance that uses virtuosity only in the services of "poetry," not as acrobatics misconceived as art.

Dance that does not separate sacred and profane.

Dance that knows dance is a metaphor of existence.

Dance that can paraphrase the ancient Hindu saying, "Let those who dance here, dance Him."

Dance that knows dance is, should, and can be a way of saying now.

What is modern dance?

Modern dance came into existence roughly in 1927. It had to come into existence. It brought a new physicality, a refreshing destruction of the lifeless, two-dimensional theatre, a more beautiful and comprehensive technique, and the first successful vocabulary for mature ideas in the Western world.

And it is not so much that it already has been done. It still has to be done!

When I was a green and frightened kid at Harvard and very unsure about becoming a dancer, I had a young sweetheart who fitted her beautiful name of Gabriella like a glove. Once we danced practically all night at the Copley-Plaza Hotel in Boston. The next day she told me I danced like a young deer. That extravagant and perhaps undeserved compliment was never forgotten. It always challenged me with the problem of the modern dance technique.

Old ways of doing things pall on alert artists and alert audiences, especially when the old ways prove inadequate. "The business of Art . . . is to live in the actual present, that is the complete actual present," says the impeccable Gertrude Stein.

Just because ways of expression and methods in art have produced fine results in the past, the alert artists today cannot hang on to them out of adoration or safety. Ralph Waldo Emerson reminds us that "God offers to every mind its choice between truth and repose." Once the glimmer of new possibilities appears, the art—any art—has to change.

Yes, Martha Graham and Louis Horst's "Primitive Mysteries" and "Frontier" had to come into existence.

Now, this change in any art cannot be just a "modernizing," the way façades of old buildings in New York are altered to look modern. That is not modern architecture. Modern ballet is as phony as modernizing Greek architecture.

Once Isadora Duncan had danced without shoes, without toe shoes, without a tutu, the toe shoe and tutu were dead for us in America.

Modern dance is a larger technical principle than all previous Western dance—scientifically more accurate, aesthetically more ready to express "the complete actual present." It is not a pocket of movement with a few gimmicks, a few personalized gestures which you go to a studio and "pick up." *And it still has yet to be done!*

Just because there have been lots of "modern" dancers who are badly trained, artistically inept, and untalented does not invalidate the principle. The movement vocabulary of a well-trained modern dancer will, by definition, include any aspect of movement which ballet has used previously, that a choreographer with a really modern aesthetic conceivably would wish to use. The stumbling block to understanding this is that bright modern dance choreographers choose aesthetically not to indulge in clichés of technique. They wouldn't be caught dead putting entrechats or ramrod pirouettes into their dances, just because of the boredom of doing or seeing things that everybody has seen *ad nauseam*. After "June" has rhymed with "moon" a thousand times, you just can't use it anymore! Ways of presenting the "poetry" of any art on the stage wear out, and fast, and new ones must be found. Excitement is a very fragile thing. It is that difficult "complete actual present."

When I was about ten, we had a large round dining table. Under it, I built a little model that had a stage floor and proscenium opening with a curtain which I pulled up and down with strings. After dinner, in my theatre under the dark table with a mirror, I could catch the light from the next room and light up my stage with a spotlight! I was wild with excitement. The challenge of the artist is to keep that flawless caliber of excitement impeccably new and fresh and so undying.

A human body has only two legs. Watteau had to use colors and shapes to paint, just as Mark Tobey does. How you use your given elements makes the differences in art. Just because classical ballet has used certain movements doesn't make them "ballet." They are human movements in use all over the world. The Watusis use big pliés in the second position of ballet terminology; the Cambodian dance uses predominantly fourth position; the Bharata Natya of India, the oldest tradition of dance in the world, uses third position of ballet as its preliminary position. All movements that can be used afresh will be incorporated in the comprehensive training for a modern dance, but in connection with a totally new principle of movement and aesthetics.

There is still the challenge of humanly moving more beautifully than we in the West have ever done before!

Maturity is not a traditional compliment for dance. Somehow, we have connected dance material with something adolescent and light and the step to trivial is very short.

When, as a very young dancer, I first danced in Martha Graham's "Letter to the World," I knew in my heart and intelligence that this was a more mature statement in dance than had ever been done in the West up to that time. When a few years later, I saw José Limón dance in Doris Humphrey's "Lament for Ignacio Sanchez Mejias," I knew our American dance was reaching a maturity.

The most treasured compliment I received was when preparing my dance "Stephen Acrobat" (1947) for its first performance. My poet/collaborator Robert Richman said to me, "This is the first metaphysical dance." But a Jacques Barzun realizes that this maturity need not be "seen" by any general audience any more than the average Museum of Modern Art trotter sees the ideas of Picasso's "Guernica" to any extent or can read J. D. Salinger's "Seymour" and get it. However, the works stand.

At this level, the confusion arises in the public mind by its still expecting dance as an art to stay on the level of entertainment, because it occurs in the theatre which generally requires a number of people for successful acceptance. The enlarged vision of some artists of modern dance was and is to create the most mature works they are capable of and to trust that enough of an audience will come.

The artists of modern dance know, along with philosopher Jacques Maritain, that "virtuosity is an escape for the artist." Once, after a performance of José Limón's company to which members of the Bolshoi Ballet came while they were in America, I said to José in his dressing room, "José, our misfortune is that due to the newness of what we are doing, and to the aesthetic choices we have made, no one has publicized our virtuosity, for it doesn't flaunt itself every other moment while we are dancing." Virtuosity can be delightful when it is not crass. The beautiful virtuosity occurs when it is concealed, that is, when it exists only at the service of the "poetry" of the art.

The direction of discovery called modern dance can be inept, it can fail, it can flounder, it can compromise, it can be not very bright, it can lose its impetus and courage, but it has to exist. It will not be swallowed by the old nineteenth century European ballet foisted on America, because a larger principle cannot be included in a smaller one, a salmon cannot be swallowed by a goldfish.

T. S. Eliot wrote in "Four Quartets":

There is only the fight to recover what has been lost
And found and lost again and again: and now, under
    conditions
That seem unpropitious. But perhaps neither gain nor loss.
For us, there is only the trying. The rest is not our business.

Emerson wrote:

The experience of each new age requires a new confession, and the world seems always waiting for its poet.

Gertrude Stein wrote:

Duret looked at him kindly. My young friend, he said, there are two kinds of art, never forget this, there is art and there is official art.

What were you attempting to do in your dance, "8 Clear Places"?

Each of the eight sections of the work has a title. After the title is stated, each dance becomes a ceremony of awareness.
Violent clarity.
Seeing and hearing at the same time.
Beautiful collaboration in poetry for costumes, masks, and rain sculpture with the most beautiful collaborator of stage designs, Ralph Dorazio.
Making the act of performing the music more human than ever.
Seeing the music.
Hearing 101 newly invented instruments of glass, wood, metal, skin, and paper.
Sensing duration between events of timbre.
Beautiful collaboration of sounds for north star, pine tree, rain / rain, cloud, sheen on water, inner feet of the summer fly, they snowing, squash dances by the most inventive, most sensitive, most future opening collaborator of music for dance, Lucia Dlugoszewski.

On the technical side, what do you think are the differences between modern dance and ballet?

One June night at college, when we were driving around in the bright moonlight with some girls, a couple of my pals said, "Let's go swimming in Walden Pond, around on the side by the railroad tracks where no one will see us." As all aquiver we started to wade naked into the water, for the first time I knew how wondrous and mysterious and beautiful the human body was.

43

It was what we think is the body that's the heart of the matter.

When one speaks of the difference between an art as developed at a certain historical time of the past, and a "new art," one automatically means that there has been a change of principles. Not only does the new work "look" different from the old, but it *is* different in essence. Once Baudelaire, Rimbaud, and Mallarmé had written, we started to have "modern poetry." Their poetry *was* very different from that of Gautier or Tennyson.

The transition from the "old" to the "new" in some ways "slips," but in general there is a "clean break." The clean break occurs when some individual artists, or two or three at the same time, crystallize in their conscious knowledge, their intellect, and their intuition a real shift of principles. Sometimes the clean break has to be very clean.

It is no accident that the first clean break in our Western dance tradition came through Isadora Duncan, born in San Francisco.

It is very clear from her writing, from drawings and photographs, that she intuited, more than consciously knew, a principle about human movement that Western ballet did not know, and doesn't know to this day as far as its teaching of technique is concerned.

It is scientific knowledge today, which Isadora embodied intuitively, that human movement starts in the pelvis and spine and not in the legs and arms like a marionette. Of course, fine ballet dancers never reach that caricature, but the flavor is always there.

The most beautiful human movement always starts in the center of the body, the pelvis and spine, and flows out into the tassel-like extremities, the legs, the arms and the head. In this center is the main weight of the body, the main foundation—bones—and the biggest and most powerful and most controlling muscles.

Ballet grew up in Western Europe (and then was taken over by the Russians) on a theoretical foundation which is now seen to be inadequate. The theory of ballet technique originated in the Renaissance and it was during the Renaissance that the mechanical, diagrammatic geometries of early modern science were developed. The Renaissance also gave birth to the science of anatomy with its absolutely static concept of the body. Scientifically, this has been superseded by the dynamic concepts of physiology. But the static diagrammatic artistic representation as seen in Leonardo da Vinci and other anatomical Renaissance draftsmen rooted itself permanently in the theoretical principles of traditional ballet technique.

It is no accident that an outline of such drawings is the symbolic trademark of the most influential ballet school in America.

This diagrammatic way of thinking of the body fitted in with the costumes, the manners, the architecture, the morals, the ideas of proportion, of mechanics, of perspective in painting and stage sets of the Renaissance. It lingers on like a mummy in the Western culture of today. It results in a feeling of two dimensions, of the static positions, and in an absence of a sensuous, direct experiencing of the body by the dancer as he moves.

Isadora knew that this old way was not good enough for us. The only image she had, or the only confirmation she could find in the West for her own personal intuition of what the human body today could be and how it could move in dance, was what she saw in representations of classical Greek art. This intuition in no way was concerned with ancient Greek ideas of proportion or geometry. Rather, it was concerned with a Greek aesthetic idea of "nothing too much." In some ways one can describe this as "natural." This sense of "natural" refers to the normative ideal of what the Western human body can be in developing its fullest potential, without imposition of any external concept or artificiality. It was also an ethical ideal and a poetic ideal.

The ancient classical Greeks, in a unique way, loved the naked human body and avoided an ascetic denial of it.

The glimmer of Isadora's intuition led to the development of what became modern dance. It is on the basis of this intuition that we have our beautiful movement future if we will.

In some fashionable dance circles, the attitude is that modern dance has come and gone, that modern dance is merely a mess of sloppy "emoting," but whether it is fashionable to emote or to freeze is merely a question of taste in subject matter. Now it seems fashionable to freeze. But subject matter is not the essence of the thing. It is how we are moving that counts, and how are we moving?

There is no point in criticizing and dismissing what has been done.

The finger has merely been pointed. And the work has just barely begun.

What makes your use of duration new?

To really sense duration would be one grand revolution in our dance, would be the new. Duration is always used, but it is seldom sensed. We either float on the emotion of the melody or, if we are "avant-garde," we ignore the sound. We can only truthfully sense duration and also the entrancing "instant," through pulse, heard or unheard. The rest is a pseudo-scientific daydream. The moment-by-moment sense of pulse is at once revolutionary and primitive, is eternal knowledge that is continually lost and rediscovered and each time must be rediscovered fresh and new.

Poet Paul Reps wrote and drew the most beautiful haiku in the English language. It also gives the most exact definition of duration I know. He drew two little feet and he wrote:

" now

  now "

It is said very commonly that modern dance students need to study ballet technique as a foundation. What do you think?

If modern dance is an art whose philosophy, aesthetic premises, intelligence, and meaning cannot create a complete technique, then it is a weak sister and had better drop dead.

Ballet training and the technique for a really modern dance art are antithetical. Their premises of moving are different. If their premises are not different, what is the discussion all about?

When I see dancers who say they are "modern dancers" study ballet, then I remember Emerson when he said: "Life consists in what a man is thinking all day."

Are we modern dancers lazy? Maybe all we have to do is go to our own studio and work hard enough within our own aesthetic framework. Maybe it takes twelve years of study as in the Kathakali school.[6]

Are we scared? Said Emerson: "People wish to be settled; only as far as they are unsettled is there any hope for them."

What do you feel about the relation of music to modern dance?

Dance as an art today in the West is still behind the eight-ball because music was accepted as an art for long periods, where dance as an art was frowned upon. In the whole history of the Catholic and Protestant churches, music was allowed in their worship, but certainly not dance. Dance was looked on as of the "body" and music generally as of the "soul." Christianity, unfortunately, has always been convinced that the soul was better than the body, and so music was better than dance.

In that way, music got quite a head start, wouldn't you say? But once dance began to be accepted as a worthy and serious activity by Westerners, the music was already there in large quantities, and when theatrical dance really got going, it danced to the tune of the music. That has led to that silly but common term, "interpretative dancing." Aesthetically sophisticated persons by now realize that it doesn't always just "interpret" the music, that dance exists right in its own vitality.

But in general, the way of proceeding was to "dance to the music." Even Isadora Duncan, in desiring to make dance a more mature art, decided to dance to the great classics. It was better perhaps than the tinkling music generally used in dancing then, but still an inadequate solution.

But the first modern dancers in America and Germany knew that to find a new dance, one had to find a new music. One of the true revolutions of the brightest early modern dance choreographers was to compose the dance first and then ask composers to write the score to the dance.

It was historically true that in the thirties, the dance needed to be given some "head." The movement had to find itself right out of the choreographers' very innards without hearing the sound, yes, the actual sound of any music. This was to give the dance the chance to have its own organic being. It meant letting the dance determine through its own logic, the length, the shape, the kinds of transitions, the development, the rhythm, the dynamics, the emotional area its own premise demanded. Only in this way, they thought, could the movement find its own freshness, its own "being." But this required finding composers who would collaborate and really be interested in making a new theatrical entity. Unfortunately, the modern dancers found few composers who were interested, and pretty soon most modern dance choreographers, due to the difficulty, gave up trying to work this way.

At the same time, there was one direction in modern dance where the choreographers, in wanting to be "profound," fell into a trap, an aesthetic trap. The trap was the idea that you could pretend to make a new art using old music. The music, as I see it, is an absolutely indivisible element of dance.

If you use music of a composer of the past, say a Bach, or a Chopin, or a Debussy, while you are dancing, you are also presenting that composer's thought and feeling, as well as structure. If that thought and feeling is an old feeling, not of today, not the feeling you would have if you were writing the music, then your dance is an old dance, not a new one. Dance all over the world is collaborative, a joint art. If you wish to have a new dance, ergo, you must have the other half, the music, new also. Now some fine modern dances have been done to music of the past, but not the best dances, and I am always disappointed and know I am not present at an absolutely new work of art.

There were and are reasons for this, sometimes economic reasons even. Generally, it is simply a lack of aesthetic awareness, intellectual brightness and love of the total art.

The first dances I composed in modern dance for a number of years were choreographed first with a complete and detailed rhythmic structure, and then the musical score was written by a composer. Whenever I later commissioned scores before the dance was choreographed, the composers were all contemporaries, working side by side with me right here in New York. Only once in my career have I composed a dance to music by a composer I did not know—dear old Mozart. (In a very early television program, until the legalities of broadcasting were known, only dead composers were allowed!)

For the past twelve years, I have composed all of my dances in the silence of my own body. I wanted to see what I could find right out of my own skin and bones, without any kick in the pants from the music—the way, maybe, a spider spins its web out of its own guts.

But, of course, since dance is a collaborative art, I could not have done this without knowing that I had an extraordinary composer ready to work with me, who would take the time to compose a musical score to my dance which would not be inferior to the choreography, who would create a second theatre side by side with my dance theatre. I wanted the collaboration of a new music for a new dance, a collaboration which would look at new aesthetic problems and solve them, and would solve problems never solved really, in my opinion, very often.

Lucia Dlugoszewski has made the most complete and inventive, most sensitive, most revolutionary, most future-opening and beautiful theoretical investigations and actual achievements of any composer collaborating with dance in recent years. Her first work with me was the score for "openings of the (eye)" (1952) in five sections: "Discovery of the Minotaur," "Disconsolate Chimera," "Ritual of the Descent," "Goat of the God," and "Eros, the Firstborn." Next came the program-length work, "Here and Now With Watchers" (1957). A year ago we premiered "8 Clear Places" (1960) and "Sudden Snake-Bird" (1961). Last summer, "Early Floating" (1961).

What do you think of the current ideas of chance and assemblage as methods of art?

Chance in composition is a contradiction in terms. It comes from a philosophical idea of the Far East, which is fine in philosophy and revealing in understanding one's life. A work of art by definition is a construction, a making. It is "convergent," not "divergent." The use of chance as a method of composition comes from an ill-understood metaphysical doctrine. Convergence and divergence are aspects of human life equally in balance, but convergence must always precede divergence. The "ego" of a child has to be developed *before* it can be denied, or transcended. You have to have a life before you can give it up.

The making of art is only in the aspect of the convergent, the putting together, the growing, the building. When you arrive at divergence, the downhill, the destroying, the tearing apart, you have passed beyond art and are strictly in a metaphysical aspect of human life, in just knowing the total of human life with the hoped-for end of complete self-knowledge.

The use of chance was an attempt, theoretically, to deny the ego in the making of art. But what turned out was very egotistical, for under today's conditions of being an artist, it was flaunted as a gimmick to point out the artist's "originality," and give him publicity. If you want an audience at all, the work of art has to be convergent. When you try to make works of art divergent, it is only a private art of one's own spiritual discipline and has no business being shown to any other person. Chance is too sacred a principle to ever be handled trivially.

Chance is a much larger principle than a method of making art. If one really used the total principle of chance, the chances are you would never get a work of art organized and put on the stage or into one piece of sculpture or in one room of instruments to make sound. Chances are the curtain might never go up—should never go up. The way chance has been promulgated and used and abused for composition is a very partial little corner of the whole possibility. I have noticed that in dances composed by chance, that the chief performer generally finds a way to "arrange" for chance to allow him to show off his biggest jump and leap when the rest of the dancers would not obstruct the view.

In other words, composers of art by chance have *tried* to make chance happen.

Why does that particular crow pick up that particular grain of corn at that particular moment?

We and all other centers of the world are in chance like fish in water.

When chance operates in the natural world, one sees infinite variety. Why is it that when one sees works done by chance, they all look so similar?

It's the height of egotism to think you can escape your own ego. The only hope of reaching non-attachment is to accept your attachment.

As the painter Philip Guston says about composition by chance, "Why do you want to give up sensitivity?"

If you want to get paradoxical about it, you have to get in there and make the work of art and *still* not let the ego interfere. Maybe that's too much for dancers! For all the Zen talk about egolessness, non-intellectuality, and accident, when a Zen-man fought with a sword, he didn't run around the barn or make an excursion up a tree, he stood and fought! Any Zen-man as artist made a haiku in so many syllables, and worked like a dog choosing the right word. If he painted a haiga, it was on a piece of paper! Art cannot by definition be nihilism. It is not a general mess.

J. D. Salinger in *Franny and Zooey:*

"An artist's only concern is to shoot for some kind of perfection, and *on his own terms,* not any one else's. . . ."

"You keep talking about *ego.* My God, it would take Christ himself to decide what's ego and what isn't. This is *God's* universe, buddy, not yours, and he has the final say about what's ego and what isn't. What about your beloved Epictetus? Or your beloved Emily *Dick*inson? You want your Emily, every time she has an urge to write a poem, to just sit down and say a prayer till her nasty, egotistical urge goes away?"

What is the basis of your dance aesthetic for the future?

Until we categorically confront ourselves with the bedrock of the material of our art—the *movement itself* and the very sensing of the movement, and this has not begun to be done, a deep new art of dance will never blossom no matter how advanced our music is or how engaging our spatial relations. With movement centered in the pelvis and flowing into the tassels, with the tender breastbone, with gravity undominated, we are on the brink of discovering a movement vocabulary that has never been done before.

The problem is still profoundly the problem of technique.

The avant-garde dance at present has been concerned with new arrangements but with old vocabulary, both early "psychological" modern and now, more and more ballet. In such avant-garde dance, the distinction between ballet and modern obviously does not exist. One can almost say the avant-garde does not exist.

The problem is still profoundly the problem of technique and vocabulary.

A pure animal man would be as lovely as a deer or a leopard, burning like a flame fed straight from underneath. And he'd be part of the unseen, like a mouse is, even. And he'd never cease to wonder, he'd breathe silence and unseen wonder, as the partridges do, running in the stubble. He'd be all the animals in turn, instead of one fixed automatic thing which he is now, grinding on the nerves.

D. H. Lawrence

The problem is still profoundly the problem of technique and vocabulary.

What methods do you use to insure visual and/or psychological communication? What do you mean when you say, "I would like to see *pure fact* occur in the dance?"

"I could see it . . . It made me want to sing and hit the lamp-posts."—*Joyce Cary*[7]

"Poetry is pure fact."—*F. S. C. Northrop*

Anyone who wishes to think or talk about art today will be going around in circles unless he has digested the analysis of and description of art in its first function and art in its second function of F. S. C. Northrop in *The Meeting of East and West.*

> Art in its first function uses the aesthetic materials to convey the materials themselves for their own sake. Art in its second function, on the other hand, uses these aesthetic materials not primarily for their own sake, but analogically in order to convey some theoretically conceived factor in the nature of things, of which the aesthetic materials alone are the mere epistemic correlates or signs.

The revolution called modern art gave primacy and emphasis to art in its first function for the first time in the Western world. It rigorously challenged our wonder faculty as it has never been challenged before. For the first time, absolutely naked and uncompromising, a miracle of pure fact became the frighteningly simple and staggeringly difficult discipline of modern artists. It is simple because we don't have to acquire it like calculus. It is given at birth. But it is of the most challenging difficulty because it is the most fragile and perishable gift we have. All childhood is dedicated to its destruction and only the most superb artist has enough skill to give it more than momentary existence. This is *still* the challenge of modern art and modern dance. Consider a dancer walking; then consider a dancer wondrously walking.

However, another observation of parallel importance to be made is that art in its second function is of equal value. The misplaced zeal of some current avant-garde artists has caused them not to understand this.

Any work of art, upon analysis, will be seen to be located either at the absolute pole of art in its first function, or at the absolute pole of art in its second function, or at any one of an infinite number of points on the sliding scale between the two polar extremes. Further, different parts of any work of art can slide to different positions on the scale between the two absolute poles.

Many people who have not seen many dances on the stage will be inclined, because of the old predisposition in the West to value only art in its second function, to imagine that a dance does and should tell a "story." Or, if they are more sophisticated, they expect at least to see some specific idea or concept conveyed. That is what people mean by "communication." They mean the "communication" of some notion of some kind that they can pretty much put into some framework of words.

That is why years ago when I first came to New York and began to see modern painting in the galleries and museums, over my shoulder, I always heard someone say, "What does it mean?" They were indicating that they were not communicated to and that they expected to be, and took for granted that they should be.

And they *were not* communicated to. Generally, it was because the artist was not trying to "communicate." That was because he was using the aesthetic materials, the colors and shapes in and for their own sake, and not trying to convey anything about anything else not on the canvas.

The revolution called modern art was going in the direction of saying that this is fine and good and important and enough. When you just look at a color and shape which refers, or indicates, or represents nothing else, no concept off the canvas, there is no communication. It is wondrous, that's all.

When I touch my cheek to the ground in "Here and Now With Watchers," it's wondrous, that's all. This is what critic Alfred Frankenstein meant when in reviewing "Here and Now With Watchers" in the *San Francisco Chronicle*, he said, "Hawkins' choreographic achievement is least simple for the reviewer who wants to convey some idea of what his work is like."

When Joyce Cary has his adorable Gulley Jimson say, "The powder puff clouds were getting harder and rounder. The sky was turning green as a starboard light. And I could see it. It came right in and made a considerable impression. It made me want to sing and hit the lamp-posts" he knows the simple and difficult miracle or art in its first function. "I could see it . . . It made me want to sing and hit the lamp-posts"!

To call, as some people are apt to do, the immediate apprehension of colors, shapes, sounds, smells, and movement a "communication," is fuzzy thinking and terminology. Coffee, when you taste or smell it, doesn't "communicate" to you. If you see the movement of an impala or a sea gull, you merely see it as the wondrous prime event, and you are not communicated to on that first level of seeing.

So it is with dance. The pure fact of movement is movement done in and for its own sake, before it refers to anything else and before it becomes a language to tell the viewer anything.

One sees then that when dance movement is presented by the dancer in and for its own sake, there is no "communication." The dancer is dancing and the viewer is seeing the dance in and for its own sake and there is wonder happening, not communication.

It is here, in finding new movement, unlike anything that has ever been done before, that the most beautiful and exciting possibilities lie before us at this particular historical time.

But this is not a crusade. This exploring of new movement, this finding, is simply a challenging matter of delight, of pleasure in the prime material of dance, the movement itself.

In the next dance which I might wish to do, I might very well use the movement of the dance to tell something about some aspect of human experience, that is, to convey some idea.

Let me explain by speaking about my dance in eight sections, "Here and Now With Watchers." The first six sections are art in its first function rather purely, that is, the dances are composed for the sake of the movement alone, for wondrousness. People who don't believe their senses, and who don't see that this *is* possible, have tried to read "ideas" or meanings into these parts.

But the last two sections, "(clown is everyone's ending)" and "like DARLING," a love dance, obviously refer to some aspect of human experience that exists off the stage and so are not just movement in and for its own sake. They are dances that point rather far toward the pole of art in its second function. This structure of the dances was made to give the work a kind of totality.

Now, if a choreographer wishes to tell the audience something and doesn't "communicate" to it, either he has not found the way to make his meaning clear, and so is a poor artist, or else the audience just isn't bright at hearing (seeing) the language, or ready, and so just doesn't understand what the choreographer is wishing to communicate. If I speak to you in Chinese and you just don't know how to understand Chinese, then there is no communication. So, too, if I speak English, and you don't pay careful attention, when I speak quite clearly and wish to convey a fairly subtle idea, you won't understand either, you won't receive a "communication."

Perhaps the challenge for any choreographer as he looks in the mirror every day is to say to himself, "When uncommunicating, be wondrous. When communicating, communicate."

How do you handle space?

Do you mean on earth or on the moon?

Artist Willem de Kooning says the space he knows exists between his outstretched hands.

Why does a man dance, and what does he dance, and who should watch him?

After I had started my first dance training, for two years I did not write to my family to tell them what I was doing. When a young man has arrived at his vocation and is put in the terrible position that his vocation in the world's eyes is a questionable one for a man, you can see what trouble he is in.

After a couple of more years of training, I took a summer off to settle this question for myself. I was born on the New Mexico-Colorado line very close to the oldest dance cultures in America, those of the Seven Cities of Cibola, the Zuni, the Rio Grande Pueblos, the Hopis and Navajos, but I had never seen any of their dance ceremonies. So I spent the summer traveling around in an old Model A Ford, ferreting out word of every dance given that summer in New Mexico and Arizona. I had to see and feel whether a grown man could dance without being a fool.

That was a wonderful summer for me, for it set my soul at rest. I saw beautiful Corn Dances at Zia Pueblo where two men, then two women, then two men alternated down the dance line from the older men at the head to the kids of four and five. Sometimes, the older men danced with their beautiful black straight hair hanging down their backs to their waist. At the Hopi village of Mishongnovi, I saw the chief of the Snake clan, limping with his hurt knee, lead the line of men into the plaza. He was ninety-two.

That summer told me that I had seen men use dance as part of their worship, part of their way of coming into harmony with their own life and the lives of all the other centers of the world around them. I saw how the men singers and the Mudheads, the clowns, watched with great care and hovered over the sacred dancers in their Kachina masks, that through the dancing the people were protected, and that the young men were initiated into manhood. I saw knowledge of divine and inner power and harmony among people.

That summer made me know that I would never be happy until I found a way to make dance for all Americans part of a concept of totality. I knew that dance would never be for me only entertainment. I knew I could never again make the distinction between sacred and profane. At the end of a two-day ritual Rain Dance at Zuni with forty-four men in masks, I had seen the Mudheads make the Indian crowd roar with laughter in ritual comedy.

Once the dance of men in our theatre is not partial, piecemeal, a triviality, mere virtuosity, mere Romantic daydream, mere narcissistic display, mere exhibitionism of private neurosis, mere adjunct to the display of women's charm, it will be honored and will be a worthy vocation among all of men's worthy vocations.

It is the specialization in our dance in which it is not demanded of men dancers that they be complete men and complete artists, carrying on their art in relation to everything else in the world, that has given dancing for men its bad name and its insignificance.

Dance for men in America has no prototypic underlying ritual and myth such as the matador in the Spanish bullfight has to give him his challenge, his commitment, his worth and his honor. But unless something equivalent to this is finally created in the soul of the American people, a man's dancing will always be inconsequential.

A man dancing will have to go far beyond entertainment. A man dancing somehow will have to stand for what a man can become. He will really have to be a hero, in his body, his mind, his spirit.

I say that when President Kennedy has to admit to the world in a public speech that seven young American men have to be drafted into the army in order to weed out two worthy to be soldiers, then something is wrong. When three of the five rejected fail to meet normal physical standards, and two of the five fail those in mental health, something is wrong, and the deep excitement of living a full human life is denied these young men through inadequate ways of developing our human potential.

Where is the image of a man fully developed in mind and body, integrated into reality, to be found more ideally than in the purposeless rhythmic play of the dance?

For dance is the most beautiful metaphor of existence in the world.

The absence of this knowledge will have to be corrected in the Western world. Sport will not suffice, no matter how marvelous it is. But even in sport, the more rhythmic, the closer to a dance, the more purposeless it becomes.

The great image of the path of purposelessness in the East is the dance of Shiva, Nataraja, lord of the dance, in the construction, maintenance, and destruction of the world. It is not chance and not inconsequential that the Western world has no equivalent.

The man dancing in America, no matter how long it takes, will have to find this archetypal image: *that the man dancing in theatre is showing man becoming man.* The man dancing in the theatre is the image of man as he performs the rite of being a man for all men in the audience, as "In each corrida the entire country is watching the reflection of its hope . . . At each triumph the matador, once more, is unfurling the map of his country. Eternally, in sacrificial blood, rises the country of Spain, the country of men."

That is not our way, but we shall have to find another way to come to the same place.

Our present conception of why a man as dancer is lightweight is a hangover, in large part, of the position of the man in ballet of Europe, and it is a great pity that it was ever imported to pollute the possible development of dance art in America. For something is wrong when the men dancing in ballet are often in the public press called "the boys." Somehow, then, they are not psychologically fulfilling the function of men in the art.

This great distortion inherent in the beginnings of ballet was that the *person* of the dancer was exhibited and *not the art*, the inner art, as seen through the dancer. It is part of the culture of personality of the West. Just as the woman in our culture was looked upon, in the words of Simone de Beauvoir, as "object," so her place as "object" was transferred to the stage. Since in real life the woman was accepted and approved as "object," so she was approved by the male audience as "object" on the stage. When the man entered the stage as dancer with its emphasis on charm and physical display, he too was regarded as "object." But in our culture, a man with a man's work to do cannot be an "object." So here was the impasse. He was tolerated because he could lift the woman and display her. If she was a princess, then for appearance's sake, you had a cardboard prince. Sometimes this rather superfluous "prince" drops his role of prince and becomes an acrobat and does some air turns and pirouettes and grands jetés. Naturally, the man can do some virtuoso stunts that a woman can't.

But a grownup woman doesn't want to see only little boys dance. Ask any psychologist about the woman's dreams of Spanish men and satyrs. Why today in America are more Spanish dancers booked throughout the country than any other kind of dance?

Not until the men in our dance find not a copied passion, but their own flesh and blood passion, will our dance be good enough, and our women take their rightful place as awakened women.

It is time to clear the decks.

How do you choreograph for a woman?

To reveal her in dance as though she were a Modigliani.
To reveal her as a Maillol and not a Degas.
To say with Saint-John Perse:
"Tu es là, mon amour, et je n'ai lieu qu'en toi."
To compose a dance for her as e. e. cummings writes a poem for her:
"The poem her belly marched through me as one army."

Five/ The Body Is a Clear Place

I

The error consists in believing that because it is possible it is desirable.

Is it not likely, in a period when many departments of Western thought (birth control, democracy, reconsidered distribution of technological wealth, psychosomatic medicine) are relooking at the basic premises of thought and action, that now is a time to relook also at the specialized art of dance and see whether a correct and complete concept of the dance art exists?

What Is a Normative Theory?

The philosopher F.S.C. Northrop states the clearest definition of philosophy—it is simply looking at one's basic premises.

To be unconscious of basic premises is to limit oneself to old patterns, areas, and processes, which may or may not be adequate to circumstances of time, new knowledge, new needs of society, new wonder, new delight, new possibilities.

To be unconscious of one's basic premises in any human activity is apt to lead only to action which is limited, clichéd, provincial, inadequate and sometimes harmful to oneself and others.

Perhaps today in the Western world, the art of dance has burgeoned as never before as a theatre art.

A normative theory in any subject proposes a distinction between *what currently is* and *what ought to be* both for now and for the future.

What Has a Normative Theory to Do with Dance?

To formulate a normative theory is simply to look at your basic premises—to look where you now are and where you are going.

Not to formulate a normative theory for any of the arts today is to allow them to do either of two things: 1. stagnate in inadequacy and dull repetition of other generations' vitality; or 2. stampede like mindless cattle down a senseless corridor into death—death for the artists and death for the audiences, their fellows whom they could be serving with life. Literal death maybe, if the intelligences, hearts, and bodies are not on the side of life.

The error consists in believing that because it is possible it is desirable.

Formulating a normative theory means deciding what you want. Having decided what you want, you have some chance of finding the means to arrive at your desire.

Where Does One Look for a Normative Theory?

One of the most important insights which Northrop makes clear in *The Logic of the Sciences and the Humanities,*[8] is that in Western thought, no area of the arts, social sciences, religion, and humanities can proceed validly without reference to the deductively formulated, empirically verified hypotheses of Western science.

The art of dance is not autonomous any more than religion. Dance cannot express untruths any more than religion can say the sun goes around the earth.

The art of Western dance in all its forms rests on certain ideas of what the human body is and its value, of what a human being is, and of what a good society is. The dance is derived from deductions about these philosophic premises. The dance just isn't in some cubbyhole vacuum all by itself. It is part of the fabric called society.

Confucious saw this when he said, "Show me the dance and music of a country and I will tell you the state of health of that country's morals, religion, and government." Any development in the art of dance from *what it is* now and *what it ought to be* must be deduced and derived on several levels, from new, corrected, and expanded knowledge of nature and the natural man as exhibited by contemporary concepts of science.

Three Assumptions that Dance Is Important

Three main elements of the art of dance require careful scrutiny to develop a normative theory today for dance:

First: The human body itself, the primary material of dance;

Second: A new exploration into aesthetic possibilities which have been ignored or belittled generally in Western art;

Third: The understanding of the psychological, ethical, social, and religious uses of dance. How these aspects of human life are used in the dance art will contribute automatically either to a positive or negative development of national society and world society. Either society affirms life as a principle or denies it, no matter on how great or how small a scale. Dance is here, is not extracurricular, is important.

An intellectual formulation such as the above is obviously not for that section of the participants of dance who are content to holler, "Look, Ma, I'm dancing!"

The Beautiful Must Be the True

Probably less than five people in America are totally convinced that no amount of dance education, dance training, dance invention, dance composition, dance production, and dance viewing can lead to a significant historical result and to a really meaningful human result today without a revolutionary change of base, concept, premise and knowledge of the scientific truth about human movement.

It seems inconceivable to ordinary folk, to the naive realistic mind, that men know how to send millions of people across oceans, 30,000 feet above the water, and yet that the principal professionals of the art of dance have not been introduced to the most simple, correct knowledge of how the human body functions in moving; that still the professionals do not realize that only through scientific knowledge, through obeying the laws of nature in human movement, can one avoid ineptness, limitation, dysfunction, and injury to the organism.

Ultimately, ugliness in the body and in movement, on the stage and on the street, is, first, ignorance of the laws of movement.

The present state of consciousness of the body, in Western tradition in dance, is as different from what it should be as Leonardo da Vinci's famous drawing of the male figure in its geometrical, diagrammatical enclosure of square, pentagon, and circle is to a living cat jumping up onto the fence. It is the difference between the static anatomy of the fifteenth century and the dynamism of modern physiology.

But even this erroneously-conceived, Renaissance-developed notion of how the body is experienced is secondary to another fact.

The scientifically investigated, experimentally verified knowledge of how the human body correctly moves in accordance with nature's law (laws as ascertainable as the laws by which airplanes fly) is the study of movement, known by a few scientists in the field of kinesiology. This correct, scientific knowledge, insofar as it is known and verified, has never been admitted nor has ever penetrated into the stream of dance technique in a complete way, in any school known by the author in this country.

Four years ago, the Erick Hawkins Dance Company gave a performance as part of the Arts Festival at the University of Texas. Dr. Hubert Lyle came backstage afterward, introduced himself, said he was a physiologist in the Space Medicine Project in San Antonio, paid a compliment (which was like having one's hypothesis empirically verified), and then chatted about movement in running and various sports.

Almost out of the blue and as a *non sequitur*, he then volunteered the observation that the theory of academic ballet is unscientific. In three sentences, he pointed out the principal error in ballet theory: namely, the erroneous belief that the body is supported primarily by the muscles of the lower back.

Insofar as kinesiology is a deductively formulated, empirically verified science, the art of dance cannot build or maintain any theory or practice which contradicts this science.

The point of this statement is that no art is validly based in its premises, nor can it avoid tumbling like a house of cards, when its theory is erroneous through the fact of contradicting anything the natural sciences know as true.

Northrop's earth-shaking insight is that all correct knowledge in the theoretic component of things (that is knowledge in philosophy, social sciences, economics, and religion) must be derived from deductively formulated, empirically verified theory in the natural sciences.

Therefore, no concept can be used as a premise in the art of dance which contradicts anything verifiable by natural sciences.

Yet, it is exactly this error of the theory of academic ballet, when it bases its physical training of the dancer's body on getting the principal support and maintaining alignment and balance by means of the muscles in the lower back, that automatically renders the whole activity invalid and false. It is the prime error which will compel the theory of ballet to be superseded.

Free Flow and Bound Flow

The second, most glaring theoretical error in all Western dance theory, including ballet and modern dance, is partly a consequence of the first error of maintaining the support of the lower back muscles.

Very soon, however, this second error is seen to come from a spiritual or psychological error, a subtle Puritanism. It is this: The spirit of Western man, as a result of his economic, social, and religious ideas, has made him think he had to work, exert effort or force, and to conquer nature. Therefore, unconsciously, from the first formal steps of training, dance teachers in the West have passed on this erroneous notion about human movement—that you must "make" the movement happen, or dominate the movement through your will or "hard work."

The acceptance of effort as a norm of movement has permitted all kinds of aberrations in Western dance art: tight corsets for men and women, an aggressive or militant athleticism which is opposed to poetic sensibility, and a sad and perverse lack of true animal grace.

The notion that the body is trained to move well through effort, through work, through domination, through "making the movement happen," through the tightening of muscles in order to do the movement, is common to theorists in academic ballet and to practitioners in modern dance, since there are no longer any vestiges of a theory in modern dance.

There is no such thing as "modern ballet," any more than it is "modern architecture" when someone doctors up the front of an old 1890 office building with a modern façade. What is really meant is "modernistic ballet." Ballet by definition is a set of principles, physical, psychological, historical and aesthetic. When these are altered by a new normative theory, you have something else, which is the subject of this essay. This is the reason that ballet and modern dance will never join theories.

The attempt to train the dancer's body in this way has led to the grave misconception that interfering with muscle action is useful, that "binding the flow"[9] builds strength. On the contrary, only "free flow,"[10] as Harvey Rochlein (using Rudolf Laban's term) characterizes the movement of the Theatre of Perception,[11] allows for continuity, flexibility, grace, and strength, and finally true, unforced brilliance.

The body is a clear place.

Effortless Movement Is Beautiful Movement

Henry Lee Munson, Jr., doing intensive work in Chinese at Columbia University, recently called attention to the ideogram for dancing. It is formed by two radicals which join in the ideogram to mean, "without effort, or opposition."

The dancing body is a clear place.

A Third Error: The Western Concept of the Desirability of Excentered Movement

A typical way in which erroneous concepts can be transmitted unthinkingly from generation to generation of teachers and writers is through quotations. In an article published in *Dance Perspectives—1,* Lincoln Kirstein[12] quotes from a book written by André Levinson in the 1920s:

> The movement of the Oriental dance is concentric. The knees almost instinctively come together and bend, the curved arms embrace the body. Everything is pulled together. Everything converges. The movement of the (Western) classic dance, on the other hand, is excentric. The arms and the legs stretch out, freeing themselves from the torso, expanding the chest. The whole region of the dancer's being, body and soul, is dilated.

This passage quite literally reveals why the theory of classic ballet is scientifically incorrect. Every kinesiologist knows that all good movement, effortless movement, is concentric. By definition, bad movement is excentric, effortful. The biggest tumble of the acrobat, the most extravagant movement of the ice skater, the antics of the clown-diver, all are concentric or they would break their necks.

The dancer trained by incorrect theory generally does not kill himself; he just injures himself and stops dancing. The reason one is filled with wonder at the movement of most animals, like the members of the cat family, is that they are always concentric, effortless; they have never been taught a fallacious theory which, out of partialness of the human mind, has inculcated ideas such as Mr. Levinson and Mr. Kirstein's that a man should glory in being excentered, filled with effort and striving, and subtle Puritanism.

A Post-Industrial Society and Perversion

A further error in dance technique is the attractiveness of perversion.

Only efficiency in movement can be called the starting point for the development into the beautiful, except by a perversion of logic, reason, simplicity, perception and sensing the suchness of things.

When concerned with the primary material of dance—the body and the way it moves—dance theory must not only encompass correct positive knowledge, but must also evaluate human perverseness.

THE ERROR CONSISTS IN BELIEVING THAT BECAUSE IT IS POSSIBLE IT IS DESIRABLE.

The machine tyranny of the nineteenth-century industrial society has distorted the totality of insights into the human body and has brought about a whole culture of perverse consequences, both physical and psychological, as a result of its partial and rigid points of view.

The nation now is really in the midst of twentieth-century, post-industrial society, but it will take courage to face this truth of its historical position. One must give up, once and for all, the worn-out, nineteenth-century science fiction seduction of art caught in the snares of technology and face the body in the new liberated truths of the twentieth century.

Intuition must begin to look toward a vision of the human body in its most harmonious perfection. This vision of the norm of the most fully developed human body—the most harmonious, the most organic, neither too much, nor too little—is probably unconscious in everyone.

But the only Western society which placed the beauty of the human body among the highest values of the good life was the Greek society of the classic period. One of the probable reasons it is called classic is that then there was the most highly cultivated love of the human body.

It was because European ballet was so antithetical to this vision of the body that Isadora Duncan castigated it so violently, and that certain artists at the turn of the century found her at least a partial expression of this dream of beauty of the human body. Forty years have passed since her death. An honest evaluation of her vision and the impetus of her ideas shows she was on the track of a more correct normative theory of dance.

The use of the toe shoe since 1830 in European ballet, and the transplanting of it to America en masse in the 1930s, is the same kind of aberration and perversion. The toe shoe is a machine; it is an industrialization of movement. It makes a woman who wears it cold and untouchable instead of warm and human. It offends, first because it prevents correct and truly beautiful, normal, human action. It quantifies and sterilizes movement. It is only less abnormal and ultimately repugnant than exhibitionistic contortionism.

By definition, any action such as dancing in shoes which deform the human foot is perversion of nature and contradicts nature. The most beautiful woman in the most chic Parisian clothes, in high-heeled and pointed shoes, is just as ugly and perverse. (She knows it and takes the damnable things off under the table the first chance she gets.)

Only Beauty Leads to Freedom

Scientific truth, correctness, and efficiency in movement can be the only keystone to beauty. Without this efficiency, nothing historically and mistakenly called beautiful is actually beautiful. The beautiful must be the true.

Thus, the beautiful on this first level in dance art is not defined by personal or cultural whim or precedent or usage, but by a criterion that can be recognized by any human being, anywhere.

The first level, then, is movement based on natural science.

The Body Is a Clear Place

The second level is that movement so based on natural laws creates beauty.

The third level follows philosophers Schiller and Marcuse: "Only beauty leads to freedom."

II
Revolution Is the Theatre of Perception

At this point, it is necessary to pass on from the more obviously verifiable scientific concept of the actual movements of the human body used in dance to other aspects of a corrected normative theory. Here is the most subtle revolution. This is the point hardest to talk about and most complicated to describe.

The earlier discussion about scientifically verified correctness of movement belongs more specifically to what F.S.C. Northrop calls the "theoretical component" of things.

The next subject is part of the second and complementary aspect of the world, the "aesthetic component." Deriving and developing the word aesthetic, as in "aesthetic component," to a more special use of the word, "aesthetics," according to one definition by Herbert Marcuse,[13] "is a science of sensuousness."

The Western world has paid a terrific price when it developed so one-sidedly the "theoretical component" which has led to miracles of specialization: the microscope, the invisible waves of sound, the rockets to the moon, the computer. With machines like the ice skate and the toe shoe, Western nations can quantify movement unlike any non-Western peoples. But in so doing, in dance and in daily life movement, sensuousness in the body has atrophied in the course of centuries as Western thought departed tangentially from the common denominator of human experience of all other peoples in the world.

This is why Marcuse says, "Aesthetic culture presupposes a total revolution in the mode of perception and feeling."[14]

Sensuous Intelligence versus Sensuous Degradation

To be alive is, of course, to perceive. But everything in the senses is not sensuous. The subtle puritanism, or attitude toward effort which is the desire to dominate, can result in movement obviously perceived with the senses but which is not sensuous, delicious. Sensuousness is always effortless. Through sensuousness, the body becomes a clear place.

It is possible to know the world through the sensuous intelligence. The error is in not seeing that sensuous intelligence is fragile—that it can be easily perverted into sensuous degradation.

The meaning of the word "reason" as Marcuse[15] uses it in the following passage could be made to include something more than just reason, but stands adequately for the principle:

> Civilization has subjugated sensuousness to reason in such a manner that the former, if it reasserts itself, does so in destructive and "savage" forms, while the tyranny of reason impoverishes and barbarizes sensuousness.

Tight Muscles Cannot Feel

Ultimately, Marcuse's use of the word "reason" connects with the drawing by Leonardo da Vinci of the man's body within the geometrical figures. They are both referring to the same category of how one experiences. But the inappropriate use of reason is the same as the inappropriate straight-jacketing of the human body in a diagram.

The Western approach to dance has always tended to forego sensuousness. Social, economic, theological, and aesthetic ideas have had other emphases than the sensuous way of experiencing, and so dance, by necessity, has been part of the one fabric of philosophic concepts.

If one remembers watching Galina Ulanova of the Bolshoi Ballet and Shanta Rao of the Bharata Natya, the oldest dance tradition of India, one comprehends the absence and presence, respectively, of sensuousness in superb exponents of two possibilities of human movement.

This point is the theme of Norman O. Brown's *Life Against Death*,[16] and Marcuse's *Eros and Civilization*, and of Northrop's pioneering insights in *The Meeting of East and West*,[17] in which he shows how Western civilization will end in total sterility and destructiveness without due and equal complementary importance being given to the aesthetic component of things, the immediately apprehended, the sensuous.

TOP: Erick Hawkins in
Trailbreaker, 1940. Photo
by Barbara Morgan.

LEFT: Erick Hawkins in
Yankee Bluebritches, 1940.
Photo by Barbara Morgan.

Erick Hawkins in *Free State—Kansas*, 1940.
Photo by Barbara Morgan.

Erick Hawkins in *Here and Now with Watchers*, 1957. Photo by A. John Geraci.

Erick Hawkins in "Pine Tree" from *8 Clear Places*, 1960.
Photo by Dan Kramer.

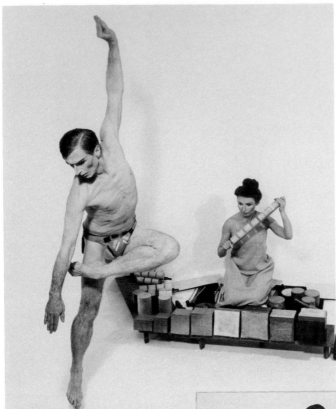

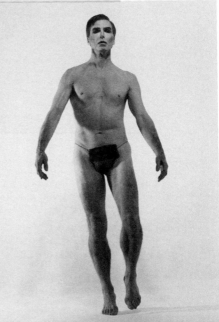

TOP: Erick Hawkins and
Lucia Dlugoszewski in
Geography at Noon, 1964.
Photo by Michael Avedon.

RIGHT: Erick Hawkins in
Naked Leopard, 1966.
Photo by Michael Avedon.

Erick Hawkins in "Thunder" from *Black Lake*, 1969.
Photo by Ted Yaple.

Erick Hawkins as John Brown in *God's Angry Man*, 1945.
Photo by Michael Avedon.

TOP: (Left to right) Erick Hawkins, Randy Howard, James Reedy, and Mark Wisniewski in *The Joshua Tree, Or Three Outlaws,* 1984. Photo by David Fullard.

BOTTOM: Erick Hawkins *(background)* and Cynthia Reynolds *(foreground)* in *Death Is a Hunter,* 1986. Photo by Martha Swope. Copyright © 1986 Martha Swope.

Erick Hawkins in *Ahab*, 1986.
Photo by Peter Papadopoulos.

The wonderful importance of these three contemporary thinkers in America is that they now make sensuousness of equal value with the intellect. The new revolution is in neither form, nor content, nor in the titillations of chance. It is in sensuousness, the true Theatre of Perception.

Sensuousness is effortless and has no sense of the dominating exhilaration of competitive achievement, nor of the morbid excitement of aggressive violence.

Sensuousness is impossible with tight muscles. Tight muscles cannot feel. Only effortless, free-flowing muscles are sensuous.

Subtle Puritanism

Existing techniques, both ballet and modern dance, are bound by a subtle Puritanism that is rooted in effort and work, as opposed to play. Both Brown and Marcuse show that the psychological reasons for this are basic egotistical fears involved in anything one does not dominate.

Clearly, sensuousness is impossible without a revolution in movement technique.

In her autobiography, Isadora Duncan tells of watching Anna Pavlova in Russia during a warm-up and rehearsal. She remarked that Pavlova worked too hard. Photographs of Duncan and Pavlova make it perfectly clear, as one looks at the coenesthesia of the two dancers, what Duncan was talking about. Isadora did not squeeze out the sensuousness from her muscles by a mistaken theory of how dance should be danced, by over-tightening muscles and mistaking the norm of muscle action.

In every photograph, Duncan looks sensuous and beautiful. Pavlova looks dry and a subtle puritanism suffuses her expression. In Pavlova's autobiography, she tells how hard she worked. She lacked play and expressed competitiveness.

Tight Muscles Cannot Feel Or Love

Without the effortless sensuous component in free-flowing muscles, people dancing together seem psychologically ugly. This becomes an especially hopeless situation in expressing love between men and women. When tight muscles cannot feel, people become solipsistically autonomous. The most loving experience in the practice of my art, and one of my greatest dancing enjoyments, is the dancing with my company, and I begin to think that this is because our prime concern with eliminating tight, unfeeling muscles spares us the tragic autonomousness.

The Function of Beauty Is to Heighten Perception

Traditional Oriental dance knows that doing must be balanced by not-doing.

The principle of effortlessness must be a capital one in a correct normative theory. No Western speed, power, or subtlety can match the brilliance of movement in *aikido* or Japanese swordsmanship, or the subtlety of the dance of the four men in "Bugaku."

Westerners are beginning to learn. Marcuse[18] quotes Baumgarten:

The principles and truths of sensuousness supply the content of aesthetics, and "the objective and purpose of aesthetics is the perfection of sensitive cognition. This perfection is beauty."

Marcuse[19] himself continues:

Nature, the objective world, would then be experienced primarily, neither as dominating man (as in primitive society), nor as being dominated by man (as in the established civilization), but rather as an object of contemplation.

Right here is the most beautiful dance—the contemplation, in the theatre, of nature in man. The function of beauty is to heighten perception, as they say the color of a flower is to attract the bee. This heightened perception makes the body a clear place.

A society's concept of nature, therefore, automatically determines its use of art. The idea of domination has pervaded the dance of the West in its attitude toward training the body and sensing the body. Consequently, it has obscured possibilities of sensibility right in the dance material; for example, rhythmic perception, dynamics perception, phrasing perception of "sculpturing time," and especially kinesthetic perception—the sheer sensation of moving (impossible with tight muscles).

In the Theatre of Perception There Is No Alienation

Harvey Rochlein,[20] in *Notes on Contemporary American Dance*, comments:

> In attempting to analyze what the Theatre of Perception exactly communicates, one finally realizes that it simply communicates wonder. Perception draws on the roots of experience that rediscover a kind of purity or simplicity or innocence, if you will. Perception is probably the dimension of all art most exactly poetic. It is neither action nor abstraction. It is personal without being personality. It is concrete rather than abstract, concrete, direct, and immediate.

Sensuousness is living in the now, in immediacy; therefore, there is no alienation. Here the body is a clear place. Sheer living is immediately experienced through one's own physical being in the very tasting of the total feast of the world around. One cannot do this through the intellect, which is always mediate, or about living and not living itself.

One can only do it through the sensuous aesthetic intelligence and this is all that perception implies. This is the great and unique contribution of the artist, to liberate one intellectually and psychologically in order to enjoy the true Theatre of Perception which is, most of all, the sensuous moving body. This is why most sophisticated contemporary philosophers feel sensuousness is so important.

III
Neurotic Is Autonomous

One of the most remarkable errors of modern times is the notion that the arts, and so the dance, are autonomous departments of activity. This is a direct result of the unwillingness of the medieval Roman Catholic Church to break from Aristotelian science and philosophy and accept that of Descartes and Newton. This reluctance divorced science from both Catholicism and Protestantism. Ultimately, as a consequence, it divorced art from religion.

This led the artist in the Renaissance to start the downward path of thinking that he originated ideas. It led to the conception of art as personal, egotistical expression primarily, and the artist as autonomous. Indian artist Coomaraswamy sums up the common Western notion of art since 1500 as the "expression of the artist's private emotional storms."

Such a notion leads in a direct line to the contemporary period, since World War II, when the search for newness at all costs for the sake of attracting attention to the individual ego has led to the greatest bunk and degeneration of all artistic values in the history of the West. This newness was exploited as a commercial commodity in a period of great upheaval of populations and the appearance by the millions of newly-educated and newly-rich groups of society.

In all of the arts today, and certainly in dance, the problem Socrates wrestled with is still with us. The problem is whether in a good society the artists will be allowed, regardless of consequences, to tell lies about the gods.

God, Man and Nature

Since the breakdown of the unity of knowledge in the Renaissance and the rise of modern science, the artist began to assert that he could legally and morally do whatever he wanted to. Safeguards against this carrying of individual responsibility into license have broken down almost completely today.

Most of the time, the artist today considers himself completely autonomous. It is Norman Brown's recent brilliant insight that only the neurotic is autonomous, trapped in the alienation of his self-centered ego. This is really what "doing your own thing" means.

What Exactly Is Art in Its Second Function?

The error consists in believing that because it is possible it is desirable.

It is here that the most important formulation of aesthetics in the history of Western philosophy, that of Northrop[21] in *The Meeting of East and West*, takes on great significance and makes possible some clear thinking:

Art is always working with immediately experienced materials which may be used in two ways. The first usage has been called art in its first function; the second usage, art in its second function. Art in its first function uses the aesthetic materials to convey the materials themselves for their own sake.

In this way, Northrop can say "poetry is pure fact." Only these aesthetic materials for their own sake, if truly sensuously understood, have the gift of living experienced immediacy, of dazzling direct reality.

Art in its second function, on the other hand, uses these aesthetic materials not primarily for their own sake, but analogically to convey some theoretically conceived factor in the nature of things, of which the aesthetic materials alone are the mere epistemic correlates or signs.

What this means is that dance, as an art in its first function, is presenting movement in and for its own sake, the pure fact of movement. But with the gradual shifting of a cloud's shadow on the side of a mountain, this presentation of the pure fact of movement starts to convey some idea of human experience not directly experienced on the stage.

Neurotic Means Partial

Here is the amazing and terrible moment! It is when the dancer is presenting his movement in the theatre in the same way that the colt runs across the field (art in its first function), and if his movement has learned to obey the laws of nature, he can tell no lies!

But the minute he starts to "communicate," to "tell" any idea, not directly in his movement, but told from his mind, at the drop of a hat he can start to tell lies!

He can start to tell lies about man, nature, man's relations to nature, and himself as part of nature. He can fall from Paradise! When the dancer, as artist, can start to tell lies in his art, he becomes responsible to his fellows, just as does each citizen as an individual in society.

Without recognizing what art in its second function means, that it is art when it uses the aesthetic materials not in and for their own sake, but analogically to convey the theoretic component of things, one does not actually understand that when the artists, including the dancer, uses art in its second function, he is *always* "saying something" or "communicating."

It is here that he cannot indulge in eccentricity—off-centeredness of the soul or of the mind—and in partial truths of his own separate self's limited knowledge.

He must take his cue from, first, natural science, and then, philosophy, and subsequently, all the departments of knowledge which are generated from the broad conceptions of philosophy, whether this be morals, religion, economics, political science, social science, biology, physiology, or psychology.

The demand on the artist and the dancer as artist, is that when he communicates in his art, he must convey to his audience only wisdom and truth. It is here, in the proposal for the third category of scrutiny in a correct normative theory of dance art, that it will meet with the greatest misunderstanding and resistance.

When Coomaraswamy contrasts the traditional Oriental way of art, even theatre art (and by this he means to include other non-Western traditional arts like those of the Navahos, Hopis, Zunis and Rio Grand Indians) with Western art, he says that the general Eastern goal was to lead the audience to "liberation." In other words, to spiritual wisdom and knowledge, hence the way the world is.

Secular art means forgetting about what the total world of man, nature and God is and dealing with totality in a partial way, leading to triviality and naive realism.

Sacred art always reveals the health of the world and all relations in it. Sacred art is always only positive, never negative and so never neurotic. Neurotic means partial. Even Greek tragedy, before it decayed (that is, became secularized), always was sacred, for it portrayed the rebirth of the soul, never the defeat of the soul, the soul which each spectator in the theatre is.

The modern secular conception of art has accepted the erroneous direction of permitting negativity, portrayed under the guise of reporting life, of telling how it is. This is confusing art with journalism. Journalism is not art.

This error, that society can innocently indulge in negativity, will bring society to its fall.

Not "Doing Your Own Thing" But God's Thing

My life's experience is made up of the way I control my negativity twenty-four hours a day. My relations with all my associates and my relations with my students are the consequences purely of the patterns of my thought in the way I believe in growth, healthy-mindedness, harmony, health, and love.

This microcosm of mine multiplied by millions is called society. All traditional cultures know they must have patterns which transcend all negativity or partiality in the harmonious whole of life, to make little ones grow to maturity and for a continuing wisdom. This pattern of relationship is love, even the love to make the corn grow. Traditional arts and theatres and dance have always expressed pure love. Periods of greatest love and faith are the periods of the greatest creativity in art.

Formulating this third aspect of a normative theory of the art of dance will show that the use of the art for private indulgence by exhibitionists and sensationalists for pandering to trivial fashions, for pseudo-science, for smart-aleck leg pulling, or for commerce, is only decadence.

This is doing your own thing, instead of God's thing.

Instead, the dance artist in this respect must be a priest, presenting the noblest concept of what it is to be a man and a woman on this earth in all the fullness of body, mind, and heart. But why should the artist translate ideas of sciences, humanities and religion into the materials of art? Many contemporaries feel this is redundant and needless.

Art in its second function is necessary and complementary to art in its first function because mediate disciplines (philosophy, science, all aspects of thinking) create entities in the culture which cannot be experienced immediately and so produce one kind of alienation. Ideas are not *experienced* directly, immediately. Ideas are mediate, about reality, not reality itself. This is undoubtedly the source of such psychotic boredom in contemporary culture.

Even a very knowledgeable scientist does not experience his ideas. He knows about them, but does not experience them.

Here, then, is another unique responsibility for the artist to eliminate this alienation and maintain vivid living cultural excitement by transforming materials, so that all can experience them directly with love.

Because many Western artists have not understood this responsibility of bringing pure sensuous immediacy to the rest of the body of human endeavor and, although handling important ideas, have rendered them with deadly literalness and naive realism, other bright artists, especially in the twentieth century, have concluded that this should not be done at all.

Ultimately, all art in its second function has only one grand aim and purpose. Most of the subjects, ideas, and themes of art in its second function are useful when honest, but still are not prime. The complete grand purpose of art in its second function is to express for the commonality of the audience, for the "common man" of the audience, only prime metaphysics, but clothed in a Theatre of Perception, in sensuous materials, of direct living reality.

Coda
The Function of Beauty Is to Be True
Is to Heighten Perception
Is to Love

When one thinks intelligently of the future, one can only think of discovering and understanding principles, or in other words, of formulating a normative theory. Any other kind of future is for astrologers. In the search for a normative theory for dance, three functions of beauty are seen.

First, the function of beauty is to be true.

Ugliness in the body and in movement is primarily ignorance of the deductively formulated, empirically verified, natural scientific laws of movement, now called the science of kinesiology. Current scientifically verified movement theory shows correct movement as concentric, effortless and free flowing.

Beautiful movement is true movement.

Second, the function of beauty is to heighten perception.

Revolution is bringing sensuousness into equal complementary significance with the intellect. Revolution is the Theatre of Perception, for only it leads to pure poetry. Sensuousness is the only living in the now, in immediacy. Beautiful movement is heightened sensuous perception of the sheer sensation of moving.

Third, the function of beauty is to love.

The Theatre of Perception will be complete only when art in its second function is understood and appreciated as a total possibility of art. Art in its second function is liberation from negativity.

Negativity is partiality as compared to the total world of man, nature and God, the harmonious wholeness or reality. This harmonious relatedness in the wholeness of reality is the concept of love. This is the complete grand purpose of art in its second function, its only possible invariant subject matter: Telling the whole truth which is love, but telling it in the only possible manner which is with love, that is, with one's most real self and totally with playful effortless sensuousness.

Beautiful dancing is then, finally, always about love told with love which is with the most heightened perception, with effortless, free flowing muscles that can both feel and love.

Having carefully and comprehensively considered a correct normative theory of dance, one avoids the absurd error of thinking that what is possible is synonymous with what is desirable.

One has returned more simply to pure, disinterested contemplation of the world and nature as Marcuse noted, and as expressed by Toju Nakae, the Japanese sage and poet: "The natural state of man's mind is delight."

The urgency and compelling force of the search for the Theatre of Perception is the sharp explosiveness of now and into the future. Each day becomes a more deeply happy one in the discovery:

The body is a clear place.

Six/ My Love Affair with Music

December 1967.

have been called a "loner," a rugged individualist, and a fool because I am one of the very few choreographers and dancers who never has and never will use records or tapes for a live dance performance.

What could be my reasons? I suppose I love music too much, I love dance too much, I love people too much to subject any of them to the predictable deadening insensitivity and unconsciousness of a machine. And by commissioning new works, I have certainly had the fun and privilege of working with such beautiful music as that of Bohuslav Martinu, Henry Cowell, Wallingford Riegger, Hunter Johnson, Robert Evett, Charles Mills, Ralph Gilbert and Robert McBride.

Sometimes, in critical distinctions made among choreographers, I have been spoken of as one of the few who used absolutely nothing but contemporary and commissioned music. Certainly, the bulk of my budget for new works goes toward music. But what may be entirely new or original in my approach to music is the unique collaboration that I have enjoyed with the extraordinary composer Lucia Dlugoszewski. We have created, together, two program-length works, both performed without intermission and both probably containing the most complex rhythmic structures in the history of Western music and dance. One is the seventy-five-minute-long "Here and Now With Watchers" (1957) for a man and a woman dancer and one musician playing on the timbre piano, which is a Dlugoszewski invention.

The other is the fifty-minute "8 Clear Places" (1960) for two dancers and virtuoso percussionist seated on stage playing an orchestra of percussion instruments invented by Dlugoszewski. Our collaboration also includes works for a dance company involving various combinations of dancers and an orchestra of musicians. These works are "Cantilever" (1963), "Dazzle On A

Knife's Edge" (1966), "To Everybody Out There" (1964), and "Lords of Persia" (1965).

There is also the suite of five dances called "openings of the (eye)" (1952) for solo man dancer and three musicians playing flute, percussion, and timbre piano.

There is the unusual dance, "Sudden Snake Bird" (1961) for three men dancers and a unique musical score involving only bell sounds. The work we did together called "Early Floating" (1961) is scored for a virtuoso soloist playing the timbre piano. Our work "Geography of Noon" (1964) is especially unique in that the virtuoso percussionist sits up stage center, with the dancers moving in front and around the musician.

The percussion instruments invented by Lucia Dlugoszewski were executed as little pieces of sculpture by Ralph Dorazio, who has also created sets and designs for me. There is no question that Lucia Dlugoszewski has created a new standard of music for dance in contemporary history. I cannot think of anyone who can even begin to be her equal. There is no composer who has been more inventive, more poetic, more theatrically imaginative, and technically successful in creating a true music for dance. She has also written some of the most beautiful, interesting and certainly far-out music of this decade.

How Am I Different

There are at least four reasons why music has been so totally important to my dance and has made me seem more deeply involved with new sound in relation to new movement than perhaps any other choreographer.

1. I cannot see how new dance can be new, when danced to old music.
2. I cannot tolerate the mechanization of records or tapes when used with live dancers in performance.
3. I cannot imagine new dance that is beautiful without being rhythmic, and this presupposes a new music for our contemporary dance.
4. I am involved with a new body discipline and new movement vocabulary that demands a new kind of music.

I have never been able to see how new dance can be served by old music.

We are living now in December in 1967 and we are everything that makes us what we are now. We are violent. We are bored. We are rebellious about our ingrained puritanisms. We are trying to find our way back to the body. We are resentful of the gigantic, mechanistic gadgetry we have created to imprison us. We are trying to rediscover how to play again, how to feel. We are frightened by our destructive insensitivity. We cannot seem to resolve the conflict between men and women. We cannot find our way clear of ugliness. This is what we are now, and out of all this will come our truly new dance and the dance that truly expresses us. And I fail to see how ideas in movement coming out of our life today can be served well by ideas in music coming out of the life of the sixteenth, seventeenth, eighteenth, or nineteenth century. The composers of those periods were facing different challenges and solving different problems and when we use their works for our dance, we not only defeat it, but we also insult their music.

Records Make Us Deaf

We are practically completely deaf from "Muzak" and we need even louder and stranger sounds to break through our callousness and indifference. For me, the mechanical Muzak-like sound of tapes and records will never promote new dance and that is why I will never use a record or tape for my dance concerts.

The living musician reinforces the living dancer to make the audience come alive. This is not easy to do. Both challenge the composer to create with originality for our life.

Beautiful Movement and Rhythm

I cannot see how we will escape boredom and the curse of contemporary ugliness without rhythmic movement. For me, unlike other experimental avant-garde dance developments, the essence of beautiful movement, its primal poetry, is rhythmic consciousness and so, the musical part of dance is especially important to me. I do not want to use music in an unrhythmic way and I do not want music whose orientation is unrhythmic and thus, unphysical. For me, this unrhythmic development is another inroad on our sensitivity and another path toward boredom.

Not only are we deaf from mechanically produced music, we are deaf from unrhythmic sound.

We are bored because we cannot feel and we cannot feel because we are movement deaf and we are movement deaf because we are unrhythmic.

A new dance which would not be boring nor ugly needs a new music that is not a sentimental, swooning unrhythmic mush of romanticism nor an avant-garde arbitrary destruction of rhythmic continuity. We must pass beyond gimmick, tantrum, gadget, or shock to a new theatrical alertness of instant-by-instant rhythmic consciousness in music and movement.

The Love Dance Demands New Dance Technique, New Music

As a choreographer, I have had a specific incentive to develop a body discipline and a new vocabulary of movement. It is not that I disagreed with other choreographers that existing body disciplines were not impressive and rich and far-reaching in serving choreographic needs. It is that I wanted something more or maybe actually something very different from what we had been led to believe dance could be.

In our dance art, I have always missed that indispensable excitement of physical tenderness between men and women which seems to me the very most basic material of the art of dance.

I wanted to create a truly beautiful love dance. To me, it is the most significant content and the most pertinent subject matter of the dance art and I could not find an existing body vocabulary that could satisfy my vision. For this particular subject matter, dance vocabulary struck me as cold, insipid, unresponsive, or aggressive and unyielding.

If one really loves women, one does not like to see their bodies trained to be artificial, ethereal, unattainable, brittle, narcissistic, aggressive, mechanistic, neurotic, or violent.

If one really loves men, one does not like to see men's bodies trained to be stiff-kneed, tight-muscled, effete, mannered, self-centered, domineering, and emotionally distorted.

If I am a fanatic, it is on the subject of the responsive body. I want to see love dancers on our stage. Without training that creates a responsive body, I think that is impossible. "Free flow" movement instead of "bound flow" movement is needed.[22]

The kind of love dance that I envisage contradicts the subtle puritanisms that govern our ingrained psychological ideas of effort and work in regard to movement. Rigid, tight effortful muscles cannot feel, are insensitive, and ultimately cause people to be bored and unloving.

What originally motivated me to discover a new body discipline was the desire to train the body to a responsiveness that would express that essential delight of men and women together and all the wonderful psychological implications that the success of such union implies. The resulting "free flow"[23] movement vocabulary of such body training had to have a new music, a new area of sound that was physical and playful rather than cerebral or ethereal.

Neither could it be emotionally neurotic nor sentimentally otherworldly, nor could it be mechanistic and gadget-like in the technological sense of recent developments. Every dance I now create is first a love dance, because the raw material is men and women's bodies and they cannot be betrayed! Then, the dance may or may not say something else.

A New Kind of Theatre

Choreographers have been concerned that movement relate to sound emotionally, structurally (one dominating the other or both ignoring the other), even rhythmically. But an entirely new kind of theatre can be achieved by putting movement and music together so that they interrelate entirely and totally with poetry.

When I move and the composer is silent because I have moved, when I jump high and the composer is suddenly very quiet because I have jumped high, when I move my little finger and the composer lets loose with a strong, brave clear sound because it is so important to move a little finger, these are instances of real poetic dialogue between movement and sound and this is what I find extraordinary in Lucia Dlugoszewski's music for dance.

A New Post-Industrial Period

For those of us who dare to realize it, we are emerging into a new post-industrial period and our very attitude toward the body is changing.

Dividing the body arbitrarily into interchangeable parts, either an arena on which to practice the laws of chance or to establish an ethereal symmetry, takes one away from the body, away from sensitivity. If you respond cerebrally, the head and the big toe can be made interchangeable.

But if you respond sensuously, they are very, very, very different. Dominating the body with the power of a neurotic emotion also takes one out of the body into emotional daydreams. We now want to see a loving body, a body that can play, be rhythmic, be responsive, be effortless. To the "hippie" generation under thirty, "love" is no longer an offensive or sentimental word. It is they who have adopted Norman O. Brown's *Love's Body* as their book.

In any case, consciously or unconsciously, we see the body in a new perspective and our new attitudes toward the body demands a new kind of music, a music that can play, certainly a new kind of music for dance. I would not be content with existing new music that would restrict choreography to a cerebral gadgetry or neurotic gloom. I had to have a new music specially created for a new kind of dance. In this way, I began my collaboration with Lucia Dlugoszewski.

How Music and Dance Should Happen Together

Music and movement happen together, but just exactly what happens is what determines the kind of theatre experience. It is like two people being together. One can dominate the other. They can become carbon copies of one another. One can cling to the other for support, strength, and emotional interest. One can use the other for a background to his own importance. They can use each other for distraction, to keep things from being boring. They can be so afraid of losing their individual freedom and individuality that they can ignore each other and end up, often, rather nastily stepping on each other's toes.

But there are rare times when two people are together when each one does an indescribable something for the other and yet no freedom is lost by either. For me, as a living experience, this is what poetry is all about, this resulting situation where everyone is richly, happily alert and clear in their attention and consciousness. I feel this poetry is the only thing that can really "turn anyone on" or make them "high." It has no counterfeit, no chemical crutch, no sentimental illusions. It seems to me to be the very best kind of living experience, the most satisfying excitement and this is how I feel that movement and sound should happen together.

The Bad Women of Music

Considering music for dance is like having "good women" and "bad women." Music for dance has mostly been considered the "bad women" of music.

Composers for dance have often been only the composers who didn't care very deeply about their art or weren't gifted enough to produce first-rate music for the concert hall, or they were fine composers who had no feeling for movement. Some were fine composers who distrusted the high-handed practices of choreographers who used their music badly and irresponsibly or who felt that dance would always overshadow and obliterate the music, theatrically, and therefore played down their efforts in writing music for dance.

What do I do differently as far as music for dance is concerned? Generally, choreographers have taken music already written and followed it carefully in terms of the rhythm and in terms of the musical structure (dance sonatas, dance concertos, dance quartets, variations). Some have followed and interpreted the score in terms of the musical emotion or they have ignored the emotion. Some choreographers have ignored the music rhythmically, to the extent of consciously and actively destroying the given musical rhythmic continuity.

Choreographers have taken music already written and used it as a collage either for an emotional bath in which to throw their choreography, or as a structural base to anchor their own shaky dance structures, or have used music as a plateau of distraction to bolster the waning interest of their dance, much the same as radio music serves a dull party.

Choreographers have written a scenario for a dance, which is an emotional sequence rather than an independent rhythmic structure, and asked composers to write to this scenario. Then they would fit their choreography to the musical rhythm and structure of this commissioned music. Choreographers have composed dances and then asked composers to fit music to it that would fulfill the dance requirements, but naturally, as a result, limit the creative expression of the music itself.

Choreographers have composed dances and then asked composers to write music that in no way took any notice of the dance. In such collaboration, there was no requirement other than that the music and dance started at the same time and ended at the same time. Such collaborations were deeply suspicious of encroachments on each other's freedom.

Collaboration Is Love

If I were asked to describe an ideal composer for dance, I would say someone who loves sound every bit as much as I love movement and who loves movement almost as much as I love movement and whose trust will be so complete that he would write the very best, fullest, and most complete music because he knows how very completely I love music. I have known such collaborations of love with music and words in Debussy and Maeterlinck and Boulez and Mallarmé. And in music and movement, I have had such a collaboration with the composer Lucia Dlugoszewski.

The Hope of New Music Is New Dance

This is what's different in my relation to music. Both the music and dance can stand alone and be performed independently, but both are juxtaposed and related instant by instant, movement by movement and sound by sound, rhythmically, from beginning to end. And the nature of this relating is instant-by-instant poetic dialogue between the two.

To be true to my dance materials, to find their uniqueness and essence, and to not be misled by musical material, I create the dance in silence. It is structurally and rhythmically quite complete and could be performed this way. By doing this, I cannot copy and depend on musical structure. I am not pulled by the cerebral, nonphysical, ethereal, nonrhythmic, and mechanical or emotionally blurring qualities of existing contemporary music, away from my explorations in pure and vivid body poetry.

Then, the composer faces the extraordinary challenge of taking this dance structure and creating a musical structure that relates to it perfectly, but also is an independent piece of music that could equally be performed alone. Contrary to the popular belief rooted in the "bad women of music" theory, such a piece of music is clearly more difficult and challenging to write than a piece of music for a concert hall.

With such a collaboration of music and dance, each of which could stand alone, you have a double theatrical richness that perhaps has never been attempted before my collaboration with composer Lucia Dlugoszewski.

She has not only taken my complete dance structures and created music that related to them, but she has created scores that could stand alone as meaningful musical structures for the concert hall. Her unique method related these scores to the movements of my dances instant-by-instant, sound-by-sound, from beginning to end. The non-listening callousness of much contemporary and avant-garde dance performance is in this way impossible. Here is a new rhythmic exploration that equally escapes the mechanical tagging along and the mechanistic destroying of all rhythmic consciousness in chance and indeterminate collaborations. Her music challenges the rhythmic vitality of the dancer as no other composer has done.

But her most unique contribution was the actual nature of this relating which was constantly in the form of a poetic comment, an instant-by-instant poetic dialogue with the movement. This also challenges the theatre presence of the dancer as no other music. Perhaps a Debussy in "Pelleas and Melisande" or a Boulez with Mallarmé, related with equal sensitivity to the words of their collaborator poets, as the Dlugoszewski music relates to my dance. As she has collaborated with me, I feel the musical stature of these works becomes every bit as significant as a new kind of contemporary opera. The Dlugoszewski music for my dance has been praised not only for its poetry, but for its theatricality.

Theatre is merely the underlining of living physicality. Dlugoszewski has met the challenge of this physicality, of rhythmic invention, of sensitivity and beauty of sound as no other composer and it is my good fortune to have such a collaborator.

Dance needs music, but it has been commonly held that music does not need dance. In an effort for freedom, now a certain kind of dance has decided not to need music and from my point of view, this makes them both damned. When music has lost so much of its physical vitality that concert halls are empty, we are reaching the era where not only does dance need music, but music needs dance.

It may very well be that challenging a composer with a dance structure that is involved with new attitudes of body experience on the levels of physicality, rhythm, play, and effortlessness or sensitivity can lead music into new, highly original paths away from the exaggerated cerebral, the mechanically callous, the neurotically emotional corners into which contemporary music has trapped itself. Perhaps the greatest new music of the future, the most original and most meaningful, will come from a true, new music for dance.

Seven/ Inmost Heaven, or The Normative Ideal

Lecture given at the Smithsonian Institution, 1978.

One of the most poignant of all the images of that great poet, Jesus, was his speaking of divinity as Father. Does it not touch a deep place in your heart when you read, "If you ask your earthly father for bread, he does not give you a stone." Likewise, "when you ask your heavenly father, your heart tells you the rest."

Probably one of the points most of us get caught on as we grow up is in imagining and demanding that parents are perfect critters. We need everything, and our parents are there to give it to us, we think. I blush to remember how long it took me to digest Carl Jung's wisdom in pointing out that a man or woman begins to grow up when he learns to take his parents exactly for what they are.

My point is, that as children, we want the ideal.

When you go shopping for fruit, what do you look for? Whatever happens, if you are shopping for a watermelon, you want a good one, don't you? Really ripe, crisp, and you love it really red with really black seeds! We all enjoy an "ideal" melon.

Those of us who have really paid attention as we studied the history of the world, and have read about and sensed all of the problems in man's history of finding a happy form of government, are a little surprised, maybe, when we realize we live in a country, the United States of America, that somehow tried to look hard at the dilemma of human societies, and when we realize that maybe we are lucky, that maybe the Declaration of Independence and Constitution actually pointed to an ideal in human consciousness that has not automatically been reached on the continents.

We know that our system of government is not perfect, but most of us recognize, surely, that its ideals are a treasure. Of course, they are violated, because men and women, flesh and blood, formulate ideals and violate ideals.

But at least in the United States we have formulated some

"normative ideals" of human government, with the aim that each individual should have the chance, once born, to develop to some larger degree of his capacity for development.

These quick illustrations are intended to give a notion of what is meant by the term "normative ideal."

Now there is one aspect in human relations which has seldom in the world's history been squarely faced by all parties: the relations between men and women. Right in the lifetime of everyone listening to me, there has been an enormous change in consciousness about men and women and their relationship. What disagreement still! Women opposing the Equal Rights Amendment even lack a common point of view among themselves!

I have, myself, in my lifetime watched the forging of a "normative ideal" of how the male and female components of human life are to be looked at with justice and happiness.

Have you read recently of the development of "microsurgery"? Why bother to use microscopes and more delicate surgical instruments to correct severed arteries, even severed hands?

Because we know that human life must be lived out as far as we can manage to achieve it. Are you not utterly astonished at the accomplishments of the human mind in medicine today?

Now I come to the primary subject of this lecture—the normative ideal of human movement. Perhaps I have shown you that in all kinds of ways we human beings automatically are groping toward ideals. Once human life exists, our very instincts say "Preserve the self"—live. All nature cries out, "Live!"

My task in this lecture tonight is to point the way toward a normative ideal of human movement. I feel myself uniquely equipped to speak about this "normative ideal" due to my long experience as a dancer, choreographer and teacher.

My exploration of this "normative ideal" was initiated by necessity.

It turned out that my instruction as a beginning dance student and later as an apprentice/artist was inadequate. Injuring myself through ignorance, a quite common occurrence in athletics, dancing, and daily life, I realized I had to discover the truth, to heal the injury and avoid repetitions of it.

By the good luck of straining my sacroiliac joint because my training had not taught me how to think/feel in my body, it was a little like Newton and his apple. I was thrust into a new line of thinking.

The results of this thinking I wish to share with you.

Very, very few human beings anywhere in the world are conscious of this fact—that every human being must—through culture—learn correct movement.

Author James Agee says wonderfully, "In every child who is born, no matter under what circumstances, and of no matter what parents, the potentiality of the human race is born again."

We take for granted that, because we all learn to walk, we have achieved all that is necessary. We have learned to write, to fly airplanes, even to play transistor radios in the subway, but almost no human beings have learned to move well, efficiently, harmoniously, healthfully, beautifully.

Efficient movement means acting in all the needs of staying alive, without violating the relation of the parts of the organism in strain, either from too much effort, or too little effort.

Absence of strain means that the muscles do not achieve any local motion of parts without due coordination of the whole of the body. This coordinating of the parts of the organism is what we call "grace."

Here we come to the heart of the matter. How do we know the "normative ideal" of human movement? Who tells us what it could possibly be?

Or, even, is a normative ideal desirable?

You can see that until we have some starting point in looking at the normative ideal of human movement, we can't possibly know what kind of dancing we want to do, or to watch.

Essentially, all of human history is a record of the search in human consciousness for a normative ideal. Most people want to get the best out of life. When that desire ends, we say a person is defeated.

Think of the anguish in the human race as it groped to refine its concept of religion. The ideal was stated and became a beacon somewhere deep in the heart of man, and then was lost.

Think of the anguish and slaughter among societies to find an ideal to do away with masters and slaves and arrive at democratic self-government. Do you remember the title of Erich Fromm's book *Escape from Freedom?*

But we keep trying to find health, justice, equality, growth.

My proposition is that we need a "normative ideal" of human movement. The movement of our bodies is the most intimate essence of our being alive.

But read between the lines. Of course, I can't possibly mean just the body. The body is not divided from the mind, the soul.

Until the day we die, we are going to move our bodies, our heart muscle, our diaphragm muscle, our eye muscles, our big limb muscles, and probably our "talking muscle."

Our task, then, our opportunity, is either to move this body in greatest harmony and unity with the essential principle of the organism, or to falter in degrees down the scale to self-destruction and death.

The notion of a "normative ideal" is a very sophisticated one. In its crudest form, it means simply that I want MY own wish, right this minute, just the way I want. Every human being gets the point of that—even a baby.

Human consciousness has developed quite a bit from a primitive state, when it can look at all experience and forego immediate gratification for a result that can be visualized through discrimination, impersonal thought, and the sensing of relationships that are not distorted through desire.

Finally, one realizes with a shock and surprise that most human beings never can "ungear" their observations from some immediate egotistical affirmation. Very few human beings get to the point of even beginning to look at things in some way AS THEY ARE, without egotistical interpretation.

The concept of "normative ideal" asks a person to quietly look at something in human culture and fathom possibilities that are dormant. A person who arrives at the idea of a normative ideal as a concept has to be a curious person, and full of faith—even the faith that man can be intelligent.

The word "normative" means a general standard, a norm, and hence, is positive in feeling. An "ideal" means having the imagination to conceive of a way to arrive at unexplored but sensed, larger possibilities.

The bright guys in any period or place are those who altered human culture, who saw that this extraordinary anomaly—man—could visualize things that didn't yet exist. Thus, for better or worse, man got off the earth and walked on the moon!

This visualization can, of course, turn to a negative and self-defeating path. The result is cruelty and destruction of man toward man and man toward nature.

The point of considering the notion of the normative ideal is that through intelligence you decide on ideas, actions, and processes that permit human existence to flower.

A normative ideal means a conscious, desirable goal.

Oh, ye, of little faith!

Throughout man's history has been heard a call to action—let's eliminate the suffering that seems to be the lot of man. All religion is simply an attempt to give men a way to get to the inmost heaven, their heart's desire.

One answer was: I come that you might have life and have it more abundantly.

One aspect of the abundant life is a healthy body and for that, we need a normative ideal.

But my particularized point—stemming from being a dancer—is that we need not only a passably healthy body, but we need a beautiful body.

So long as we have this carcass, what lack of imagination would keep us from cultivating the tenderest perceptions of the moving body.

I can reveal my intellectual point only by revealing my personal predilection.

From ancient Egyptian tomb paintings and sculptures, the perceptions of men have been to honor and reveal the glory and beauty of the body in visual art. I, in my lifetime, have gloried and rejoiced in the pleasure of seeing, in front of my eyes, men and women move in dance in the perfection of their bodies.

I have never known a glory more stunning, more astonishing than the movement in art of a beautiful man or woman. It takes the beauty of a man and woman to make the completeness of human life.

I must confess that because I adored the beautiful human body so much as I watched others, I had a great hankering to see how beautiful I could be as a dancer. Call it ambition, call it narcissism when it goes over a fine line, but better, call it pride in being a man, alive and using his potential, having all the fun out of having been born, and living for a while before dying.

Perhaps you can sense now, that having come this far in revealing my love of the body and its glory of movement, one has to look at the significance of a normative ideal for human movement.

At this point, it is possible to see that consciousness alone permits control. The lethargy of the human race is merely its not being conscious. Consciousness alone makes control possible—that is, fulfilling one's vision, one's desire, or, flubbing it.

The goal of my life as a dancer and choreographer has been just to find a way to the most beautiful human movement I could dream of and achieve.

My only real point in speaking at all is to say to you: Look, learn to discriminate, refine your perceptions and then maybe we would all, more or less, arrive at a normative ideal held pretty much in common.

From the time I was a little boy in Trinidad, Colorado, I have had a very definite reaction to what was beautiful. On Saturday mornings, after the house had been cleaned by my mother and sisters, my job, at six or seven, was to dust everything. The first time I was conscious of the beauty or ugliness of a man-made object was once in dusting a vase with some hand-painted, pastel scene on it, and saying to myself, "This is ugly."

You can imagine my chagrin as I walk along Greenwich Avenue in the Village and look in the windows of the thrift shops, and see all that stuff sentimentally collected for resale when I had known at six that it was ugly.

My instinctive reaction to the American design of my boyhood has seldom changed in any particular. It was the era when implicit in all design was the concept, "Nothing is too much."

My first awareness that all sense of fashion was antithetical to the good life came later when I was a little older and saw my sister's wedding. I am still fascinated with the horror of the design of my brother-in-law's tie.

Then I first saw in the East some Swedish "modern" furniture. I knew then a better and more beautiful world was possible.

So in college, one summer, I designed and built all of my furniture—modern.

Soon after, I began to sense how much more beautiful the body is naked than wearing trunks when swimming!

After I had been studying dance a while, I knew that I had to find the equivalent simplicity, clarity, directness, effortlessness, strip-pedness, in dance movement that I liked in everything else.

I learned to treasure the photograph of a green pepper by Edward Weston.

I was bowled over by Noguchi's set for [Martha Graham's] "Frontier."

One morning I was thunderbolted by Brancusi's "Fish all Alone" in a gallery at the Museum of Modern Art.

If you hang these things like pearls on a linen thread, you will see how they are strung together.

Then, I finally choreographed "vulnerable male is magic" as part of "Here and Now With Watchers," and my other solo, "pine tree" from "8 Clear Places," and I knew I had arrived at the same place.

These little anecdotes were merely to lead up to my esoteric idea that there is a "classicism" in the world of nature and of art where form takes on a "violent clarity."

that is

utterly simple

utterly without anything extra

utterly without fussy phantasms of the human mind, without eccentricities.

That, then, is what I am leading to in finding a normative ideal for human movement. The body's movement is the basic material of dance, so the dance can be "good" only when the body, as it moves, totally obeys nature, as a river from its source, as a spring in the Rockies flows until interfered with by a dam, or until it flows into the ocean. When gravity makes it fall in a boisterous rush, it does; when the need of the land is level, it barely flows.

Correct human movement is correct by virtue of one quite simply stated, kinesiologically observed, and tested principle. It is the conscious recognition and observance of this principle that has made me probably the most misunderstood and misinterpreted choreographer in the past thirty years.

The principle, simply stated, is: Just do the movement, whether it's chopping a log, or taking a cinder from a friend's eye. The end of the journey in the study of Zen in the *Art of Archery*, is to learn to permit the arrow to shoot itself.

But this is hard to get if all of one's previous ideas about movement and all life have adhered unconsciously to an opposite principle.

It is a little like saying to a drowning man, who thinks his only hope is to struggle, let go and float.

All ballet technique by conscious theory and all modern dance theory, totally without a principle as I have observed it (and that is why modern dancers proudly study ballet—because they have no theory of their own), is based on the idea that *you* have to do the movement.

This is a physical and psychical error.

This error disturbs the "classical" functioning of the body according to nature, where there is perfect harmony of all parts of the skeleton without inappropriate strain of the muscles.

Our Western way says conquer nature, force the body to do what the ego wants. In that forcing is TRIUMPH, GLORY, SUCCESS.

There is another way. It is the way of most non-Western peoples. It is the way of peoples who have maintained the sense of paradox.

Jesus has to use paradox to speak of spiritual principles. It is necessary now for Westerners to arrive at the insight, a correct physiological insight, that the human body functions correctly only through a kind of paradox. The very muscles themselves function well only through the balance of the opposite possibilities of action and letting go of action.

When this principle is fathomed, the very mood of all Western dancing will be transformed, brought to totality and completeness and therefore to the normative ideal.

Two aspects in understanding correct human movement are the theoretical and aesthetic component of all knowledge, says the wisest of all present-day philosophers, F.S.C. Northrop in *The Meeting of East and West.*

Kinesiology is the science, what can be known and verified by all knowers, the theoretical component. On this level, I was the pioneer and the only one, so far as I know, to have succeeded in using these verifiable kinesiological principles in the teaching of dance technique and in the framework of a practicing dancer and significant, meaningful artist/choreographer.

In developing this knowledge and utilizing it in technique classes, I have been misunderstood consistently from the beginning. Recently, I was told by a student in my school who graduated in dance from a metropolitan area women's college of high standing that the dance chairman, now retired, didn't approve of my teaching because the students didn't sweat enough.

Poor woman, she never understood that you have to earn the right to sweat only after a long time of learning correct movement slowly, with consciousness and without strain.

In the second, aesthetic component, the knower knows through direct perception, through intuition. It is a component developed by the East to find correct, graceful universal movement.

But just because they have used this way of knowing primarily and with thrilling results does not mean it comes easily to them. They "work" at it just as carefully as in searching for the theoretical component.

One of Northrop's gigantic insights—world-shaking—is his statement of "epistemic correlation." Epistemic refers to the Greek word for knowledge. The phrase means correlation of two ways of knowing the same thing.

A quick example:

Knowing the color blue theoretically is through its wave length; knowing it aesthetically is through intuition, apprehension, sight.

Dear listeners, just to write this out is thrilling to me.

Here is my bombshell:

Correct movement, the normative ideal of movement, what I have been searching for, will be movement of the body as known to be normative by the science of kinesiology and movement known to be correct by direct apprehension—sensing your own rightness.

No one, except at their peril, can just sense and do movement without checking it, through an epistemic correlation, without kinesiology.

That is today's crossroad.

Our old ways, for four hundred years, of sensing and training the human body in its movement in the art of dance are full of errors and, indeed, inadequate.

Our previous theories of ballet and errors in modern American dance must be modified to conform with what we can know kinesiologically. The theory of classical ballet is unscientific, as is hard-as-nails modern dance technique.

Years ago, I formulated the phrase, "tight muscles cannot feel." The leaders in dance were not believing their senses. They accepted injuries from tight muscles as normal. Mistakenly, they confused tight muscles with strength, and didn't see that tight muscles are weak because they inhibit action.

Tied to this theoretical component is the aesthetic (not aesthetics) component, by way of definition, the way of art. Errors in this aspect existed until the early 1950s when I started to find my way.

Direct introspection of how the body feels in muscles and bones and in its overall anesthesia—its common, undifferentiated feeling, sensation, tension—cannot remain unrelated to what the soul itself is feeling.

The way of tight muscles, tension, strain, violence, force, and aggressiveness in the body, registers the analogous state of the soul.

If the soul is deeply at peace, if the person is whole, at one with itself, full of wonder, full of love, it will not have to shoot the arrow. It will know how in confidence, joy and self-knowledge, to let the arrow shoot itself.

That state of the soul and the state of the body is what I would like to reveal in my dancing and my choreography.

I would have a wider audience and more chances to present my work if more people accepted these principles as the normative ideal. I am hanging on at present time until more people come to recognize that this is what they really want, too, as the normative ideal of a free people.

And now to close.

I shall try to convey in words the pearl of great price in the awareness of the human body.

It is the hardest thing in all of dance teaching to talk about, or to convey to a student. But it is quite exact. It is mysterious but not unknowable. The pearl of great price is the sensation in the center of gravity of the body, the center of the structure of the skeleton, the center where the largest, strongest, truly integrating muscles lie—in the front of the body, in the low belly, just where you could place your own right palm horizontally, with the edge of the little finger lightly above the bone of the *pubis symphysis*.

Those of you who ever saw me dance my solo, "Naked Leopard," can perhaps recall the red felt rectangle shape which covered me (in the noticeable absence of other costume), right at the place I have described as the center of the body. It was pure intuition, as I designed the costume, that led me to put the single important red area of color where my sensation of the body was centered.

Oh, you may have seen a striking photo of me from the dance, at the end, where I am walking forward. The photo shows the significance of this consciousness and I have always been astonished that the photographer could catch it.

What is not known, not understood by most men and women in daily life and by practically all Western dancers, is that it is completely possible and totally probable that this consciousness of the center in its true and maximum refinement is not automatically discovered by us. We can miss it! My task is to point it out.

How to find words to indicate this experience to you is just about the hardest thing to do in all of dance teaching. I grope for a word like correct placement of the center. It is a direct introspection of the center of the organism, whereby awareness of all other parts of the body fall into harmonious co-ordering, which at the end we term "grace."

One day, twelve years ago, as I was talking with my lawyer in his office, he said, "Erick, have you ever heard of Aikido?" 'No," I said. So he sent me a little book *What Is Aikido?* Another thunderbolt! Those Japanese.

Through concept by intuition, through direct introspection in the aesthetic component, the Aikido had formulated years before what I, too, had found out and experienced for myself. There is only one difference. The Aikido people speak of the single center as two fingers before the navel. I place it further down by a couple of inches.

How lucky, in this respect, to make beautiful dancing, that non-Western peoples had no Leonardo da Vinci to put them off the track by making them think of the human body in a partial way as a diagram, rather than as a directly experienced, sensuous instrument of art!

Perhaps the privilege and excitement of glory of our present flowering of the art of dance in America will be to understand that the normative ideal is desirable and that it will be formed in fullness by these two complementary principles of knowing human movement in the theoretical and aesthetic components.

One word of caution: the immediately apprehended, directly sensed way of the aesthetic component is the primary way of all art and so takes precedence. It is this awareness that leads to the INMOST HEAVEN, the normative ideal.

Eight/ Dance as a Metaphor of Existence

Lecture given at the Smithsonian Institution, 1979.

Have you recently read any of the new books with titles like *Humankind Emerging* and listened to the palaeoanthropologists conjecturing from the evidence of the skulls and skeletons unearthed on every continent about how long man has lived or shall we say—with a distinction to be made later—existed. Two hundred million years, or maybe four hundred million years?

When the mind begins to imagine such time, does not human existence itself become more and more mysterious?

Do you enjoy, or are you thrilled by, looking at such a long view? Or can you spare any time from looking at your daily troubles?

Do you think it is enough to handle, in your overall view of the world, the notion that the earth was created exactly in 4003 B.C. as a certain Bishop Ussher calculated? Do you ever stop to think that everyone, stupid or wise, in the Western world, up to 150 years ago, was locked in that supposition?

No evidence had appeared, really appeared, no one was ready to really look around at the evidence in the world, so that such a paltry view of man could be superseded by a vision of the world so much more mysterious, so much more breathtaking, so much stranger than Ussher's oversimplification.

To get a glimpse of the race of man that cuts through the narrow historical enclosure in this street, this city, this country, this way of wearing shoes and clothes, this way of enjoying ourselves, this way of walking, this way of moving, this way of looking at the sky at night, this way of dancing, is very exciting. Maybe it makes us less grubby, a little less like those unhappy souls one sees sometimes on the street corners of New York City pawing through the trash baskets, oblivious of the rest of the world.

In one's superiority, you think as you pass by: "What once happened to you that you thought you have to settle for this?"

Yet the next thought recognizes that these trash basket grubbers have "ascendants," as the French say, going back those two to four million years of human life.

So generation after generation, we humans are born and die. And each one says along with Shakespeare when he puts these words in the mouth of a pimp: "Truly, sir, I am just a fellow that would live."[24]

These words are a preamble, a little walk around, leading to the title of this essay, which has been in my head for quite a few years. Maybe I have lived long enough now to state my intuition more clearly.

For quite some time now, I have struggled to explore the dance art, and in a parallel way to explore the real meaning of my life, to see what it really is all about before I die.

This essay is an attempt to put the two together in a formal way, in a conscious way. Actually, they have never been separated.

But one becomes obsessed. One becomes attached to what is called, again by the French, *une idée fixe.*

The human soul seems to forget constantly. Self-knowledge, which some bright people on every continent have pointed out as a desirable good, seems to be something each one of us has to try to arrive at.

It is as though we had to try to remember to wake up, to remember to look at things, to see where we are, to read between the lines.

Maybe our presuppositions about the art of dance can be looked at afresh. Maybe the way the idea of the dance has developed in the last three hundred years in the West is not the last word. But to propose such a questioning entails a confession. Whatever I can say in this essay can be only autobiographical.

But I would like to have the courage to say it. R.H. Blyth, that great soul, has a wonderful saying:

All that can be shaken be shaken,
And if nothing remains, let it be so.[25]

We all grow up thinking that somebody knows everything better than we do. That the happy land is out there. But, finally, one learns that no one knows very much.

But that doesn't mean that some people don't actually know a great deal. Thank heaven, because if I am bright enough, I can climb on their shoulders and get a little further vision of the promised land.

But the real truth is I can't say very much about the art of dance if I haven't arrived at some kind of an attitude about the human race, about the mysterious possibility of consciousness in each human soul, and about how people living together in a society use this consciousness together in what we call a theatre art, the dance.

It seems, then, that if I am going to use the title "Dance as a Metaphor of Existence," then maybe I will have to talk about a relationship.

Where this essay is a little different, I suspect, is that I am not taking the dance as we have seen it in our lifetime, of going to the theatre as something just given, plunk!

Maybe it could be a little different. Maybe some basic premises have to be looked at to arrive at more completeness.

I guess there are lots of jobs in the world that don't engage a person's whole existence.

That's why I have always considered myself terribly lucky.

But it took me years of my career as a dancer and choreographer to realize why I was so lucky. But, finally, I saw that DANCE WAS A METAPHOR OF MY EXISTENCE!

Right away, after my first years as a dance student and then as a fledgling dancer and choreographer, I was having a good time in the art. But only after several years, and finally after suffering, did a mysterious imperative begin to nag my consciousness to seek something beyond just the fun of dancing. Only gradually did I begin to investigate what was my existence.

It may be harder to say what kind of dance would be desirable than to say what we don't want. How to develop a system of justice and freedom in a society may be harder to describe than to point out the aberrations and abuses of the ideal we visualize.

How to describe, as one human being to another, the kind of spiritual quality or knowledge our intuition and intelligence can imagine is harder than to analyze the ignorant perversity we can watch operating in fellow creatures and only by quick glimpses in ourselves.

But the point to recognize now is that we do see glimpses. All of us.

It is only on the notion that all human beings can catch glimpses that we can dare propose a democratic form of government. These glimpses come back to a notion of Plato that somehow we "know" or "glimpse," even when we don't know we know. Robert Pirsig has written a fascinating little book[26] in which he develops an insight he picked up from Plato's *Phaedrus*—that we human beings naturally have an intuition of quality.

There are not too many answers to the big questions and puzzlements about human existence which the main perennial wisdoms on every continent have been able to give, and be sure they could honestly say THIS IS IT. Oh yes, the human race has been harassed from the beginning by those egotists in every society, those bulldozers who said, THIS IS IT, and our IT is the only IT.

But you and I are alive. We're here. We're talking. We're fish. We're in the position sometimes of the Son Fish to whom the Father Fish said, "Son, I'm worried when you say you don't like water."

So we have this human existence, willy-nilly. It looks to me as though the bright guys all over the world, those who had some spunk, then said to themselves and to anyone else who would listen: Then let's have quality.

But, alas, quality doesn't come in some easy package, some quick kit. And there lies the rub. In a day of instant coffee, it is hard for some souls to catch on that there is no instant quality.

So now let me confess something. I was a wide-eyed, crazy kid who was so bright that they sent him East to college from dear old Kansas City. Every time I see the Thomas Jefferson Memorial from the plane as I arrive or leave Washington, I remember that I started out to be a freshman with two hundred dollars in my pocket and one hundred of it was the prize money for winning a contest for an essay on Thomas Jefferson. But something in my makeup urged me on to be an idealist, one of those crazy people who look on human life and say, "Well, I'm here, Brother Fish, so I guess I'd like some quality."

So as I keep trying to give you this notion of quality, I keep saying, "But what has this to do with the dance? You're way off the track."

But the next minute I say, "No, it is right on target." DANCE AS A METAPHOR OF EXISTENCE means then, doesn't it, that if the dance is to be of excellence and vitality, and if it is to be a metaphor, then we would have to consider what good existence is, or even what existence is, period.

So you can see that this is a very big subject. I guess one of the hardest things for us to get wind of as we grow up is that everything is related to everything else. We always want to stuff things into a neat little pocket, and get them set and not have to look at them. We want to get things prejudged—prejudices, so we won't have to look at the experience in front of our eyes. So lots of people say, cut it out. Cut out this intellectual stuff. Just dance!

My only reaction is to think and sometimes say, "Don't be so dumb." Everything one does in any aspect of life comes out of some deduction you have made from some beginning notion.

So my conclusion is, if you want to arrive at quality—real excitement, real intensity in the art of dance—you have to look at real quality in existence.

Now, it may have occurred to someone to question why I say the word "existence." Wouldn't the word "life" be more usual and natural?

Actually, this is a very subtle and jolting distinction. Later, I will try to say why I make the distinction, a distinction I picked up from the Frenchman Hubert Benoit.

But let me tell you the main idea. Benoit gives an illustration that really showed me how to look at myself. Say a man has worked hard in business to earn money so that he can have enough food, shelter, clothes, things for the cultivation of the mind, and then a financial crash comes. All of these things he had worked for are wiped away. So he jumps off a high building and kills himself, forfeits his existence, because of his image of what his "life" was.

All of us pay lip service at least, and some pay real homage and gratitude, to someone who just didn't take things for granted, and who asked if this quality which we have now is the best quality we could have.

But that is history. History is the story of the ups and downs of societies' attempts to find quality in human existence.

When I got to college, I was quite fearless and had an instinct for quality.

And then I had some hard times. It came as quite a shock as I began to observe people in the world and saw that they did things that are just plain cheesy, trivial, superficial, and so were using themselves way under their capacity.

This led to actions and relationships and to making things that were petty, cruel, insensitive, isolated, lonely, joyless, and crude and ugly.

Now I was so preoccupied with questions about what I saw in the world that violated my sense of wondrousness that at this time I latched onto reading people like Keats and Thoreau and Emerson and Tolstoy and then, in the course of my studies, Plato and Thucydides and the tragic playwrights and dear Aristophanes and, of course, everything about Socrates and especially too, sweet Chaucer.

Then mid-stream in college one day, My Muse, and "Ma Mort,"[27] came to my rescue and told me to walk along 54th Street in New York past a theater where there was a billboard advertising a "Dance Recital" that night. Honestly, dance was so new in America, I had never known dance was performed as an art on the stage.

Wow! When I came out all alone for the first intermission, for the first time in my life, I knew what I wanted to do. Dance and make dances.

Think of it! You used your body in its vigor, in its power, in its rhythm, in its playfulness. No mouse, you! No namby-pamby, something that sat on a chair all day.

Think of it! You were constantly enjoying music! You were dancing to music, you were making musical relationships with your feet, your trunk, your arms, your head, not just with your fingers.

Think of it! You could make designs. You could wear colors and shapes. Well, I don't know why some fancy warrior, seven feet tall among the Watusis should have such a good time dancing with a lion's mane on top of his head, and I not. I don't know why some Hopi Indian a little further west in the desert from where I was born should have such a good time making and wearing an exquisite mask representing the divinity inside his own heart or outside in the world, and I not.

I would make beautiful costumes, beautiful masks, beautiful sculptures and objects to put on the stage.

One of the terrific excitements for me was that the art of dance in the theatre was so inclusive. It combines so many art aspects.

Yes, I decided that dance, just by what it could include in using all of a man's physical vitality and prowess and sheer skill, could result, maybe, in making him a poet of the body. Well, I must confess something else which fits right in with the title of this essay—that dance would be a metaphor of existence.

This human organism, my body, my carcass, which includes this mind that guides this pencil to write this sentence, is ME!

So to dance seemed to me then to be the activity that used this basic me, the body, in the purest, most disinterested and most intense way.

Different from working, different from athletics.

Now, last summer for two weeks, while I attended an executive seminar at the Aspen Institute for Humanistic Studies in Colorado, I played volleyball for the first time in my life. It was wonderful fun. I wasn't bad, and I would love to have time to get better. But sports movement, by definition, is different from dance movement. No quarrel. Just don't confuse the two. When this confusion does occur in something supposedly called dance, the art of dance goes out the window. You just can't think "quantity" in dance, you can think only "quality" if it's really dance.

Just a few blocks from here, at the National Gallery, Jacques Maritain[28] said in a lecture, "Virtuosity is an escape for the artist." What he meant, I think, is that virtuosity, in the sense of quantity, is dumb in that it obscures the subtle virtuosity of quality.

Perhaps the origin of my title, "Dance as a Metaphor of Existence," occurred to me some years ago from the vivid experience of a performance. Sometimes when the curtain is lowered at the finish of the last dance on the program, the thought has arisen, "This performance was a chunk of my life. It was my existence on a knife's edge, focused in the confines of the stage space and focused into the duration of the series of dances."

Sometimes I have come offstage and felt, "There I was really living my life."

May I confess again that feeling has been the sustaining power that kept me dancing through long years of a kind of Sisyphean routine.[29]

For early on, I knew that not too many people were going to want to look at my dance art on the level I wanted to produce it and present it to them. So very early, I understood I would have to judge my results in making and dancing dances only by my own pleasure in doing so.

Nobody asked the priest Gregor Mendel to fuss around in his garden growing generations of peas, to understand the laws of heredity. And as I recall, at his death, his papers were disposed of by his superiors, some copies of his experiments surviving almost by accident. But he wanted to find out what he was going to find out.

So when the curtain goes down at the end, sometimes, without any formulation in words even to myself, I know I am satisfied. I have produced something gratuitously. No one asked me to, and I thank them for paying to see me, and letting me try to see if I can make my points to them. But essentially, I am my own first audience and, indeed, my own critic.

When I have put, say, three or four dances on the program within two hours, I feel I have made a micro-cosmos, a little world, and to make a pun on the word "cosmos," a little world of beauty.

I know my father died slightly disappointed in me and wondering why I wasn't the head of some big corporation, making a lot of money (for he knew I was bright). But I know he never got the clue—I couldn't tell him—as I am confessing to you—to why I just had fun dancing and making dances.

So let me say it this way. Most of the time, I feel triumphant and happy because to have danced well, inspired by my company into dancing beautifully, and to have made beautiful entities of choreography is a kind of condensing in time and place of my whole existence.

I think a lot of people aren't very conscious of what it takes to pull off a successful dance. By successful, mind you, I mean successful in my own eyes. If people applaud, that's gravy!

The fun of a performance for me is that I have to place a magnifying glass covering the dance on the stage under the sun of the theatre audience. Everything that I am has to be concentrated into those few minutes that the curtain is up.

One of the most terrible traps any one of us can fall into is to imagine we can hold on to anything. Because the human mind can make concepts, can reify (this is make a "re," a thing, of something that is not a thing, and to fix something that is fleeting, and to fix, even though we kill it), we can't bear to have something and then have it taken away from us.

This was illuminated for me most vividly one day, years ago, from reading in traditional Hindu mythology about a demon named Hold Fast.

We human beings have never come to a very clear understanding that our human experience isn't as the jargon is today, Hardware. Our existence, is oh so Tender Ware.

The performance of a dance is such a vivid example of Tender

Ware. Absolutely as quick and passing as the "flirt of a bird's wing."[30]

Have you ever waited backstage for a dancer to take off his makeup and watched how fast the sets are taken down and put away, the stage curtains lifted, the theatre seats emptied?

Where's the dance? Not a rack left behind! An "insubstantial pageant."[31]

Where's yesterday?

The dance is something you can't take with you. That strange and great poet, Jean Cocteau, says that if you want to see Death just keep looking in the mirror.

So let me confess again that it is a great challenge when performing a dance, to get quiet enough inside, even when your legs and arms may be flying around, just to exist and know you're existing. One of the signs of a master of any skill or any craft is that he knows he knows. When visitors to the oracle at Delphi asked, "Who is the wisest man in Greece?" the oracle answered, "Socrates." Well, when Socrates was told what the prophetess on the tripod had said, he answered, "Well, if I am, it is because I know I don't know."

So there have been several places in different dances where, in my choreography, my intent was to bring to a boil my intuition that the high point of our being alive is that moment when we know we are just existing. And strangely, in some ways it is the hardest thing in the world to do.

So in the frame of a work of art, I tried to see if I could make a metaphor of just existing, right in the dance as a plunge into the heat of the fire. Or maybe I was gaining immobility by getting right on center of the spinning axis.

The first time I did something like this was at the end of "Here and Now With Watchers," a dance I first did in 1957. Maybe some of you might have seen this dance with its marvelous score for timbre piano by Lucia Dlugoszewski, one of the unrecognized landmarks of twentieth-century music.

The curtain doesn't go down for an hour and fifteen minutes. At the end of the last dance, a love duet, "like DARLING," after my sweetheart exits, I stood dead center downstage. The music had become silence. I was tired from almost a solid hour of straight dancing.

I stood there, still. Sometimes, I was aware of my beating heart, sometimes I could see in the darkness the faces of the watching audience, the watchers, and when finally I took time to know that I was alive and that was enough, I almost coolly turned and walked off the stage to one beautiful *szforsando* note on the piano.

Another time, I used the standing still as a metaphor of existence within a dance, which itself was an example of the theme of this essay. It is the second dance in "8 Clear Places," my solo, "pine tree." Now how can you dance a pine tree?

But there is something more important than that.

In fact, the most important thing in all art is HOW CAN YOU REALLY SEE a pine tree, I mean really see it, see it as if you saw it for the first time.

You may not realize it, but we only think that life is dull and boring and that the art in front of us is just as dull and boring. But it is not life itself and not the art that are boring. It's our seeing, our sensing.

That is the reason for metaphor—to crack that boredom in our minds. Our prosaic linear language that gets practical affairs done—what philosophers Whitehead and Northrop call "naive realism"—with its short cuts, kills the life inside, that existence that I have been telling about that is luminous.

Annie Dillard said it marvelously: "Muzzle the commentator!"

Well, after the movement metaphors of pine tree in the dance, my next to final metaphor is to stand on my one green leathered leg, with the other bare leg lifted along the green thigh. I waited there until the audience could see I was a clear place just standing there as a pine tree and then in eight circles, I walked off.

That was in 1960. In 1975 at Carnegie Hall, I premiered "Death is the Hunter." There, I used a bold metaphor, not the same as "Here and Now With Watchers," or "pine tree," but comparable. I tried to use existing on stage in the actual performance as a metaphor of "existence" itself.

In "Death is the Hunter," before the orchestra on stage starts playing, I enter as Death with my beautiful mask and six-foot bow by Ralph Lee and purple robe with a black accordion-pleated paper train that slowly scratches the floor. I knew that opening night, that in my walk in the silence that takes about five minutes, that I made the audience "hear" their existence.

In reacting to this dance, some people felt I created a new time sense on stage. I think I did, because when you hear yourself existing, suddenly there is no past or future. There is an eternal stillness—something Wittgenstein understood—an endless infinite now.

I am now approaching one of the subtlest insights, I think, that I could possibly share with you. It is the heart of the matter. I think it is one of the several reasons my choreography has always aroused such controversy.

Note that the title of the essay says, "Dance as a Metaphor of Existence," not "Dance as a Metaphor of Life." Dr. Hubert Benoit's *The Supreme Doctrine,* one of the most important books of our time, elucidates this distinction. The distinction between living and existing carries to some intuitions about the dance.

You can see perhaps, or intuit, that when I was standing at the end of my solo, "pine tree," (in "8 Clear Places,") and just existing, I was not trying to express myself.

When just existing, I am in no way involved in any kind of power play, or game of domination.

Because of our various psychological vulnerabilities, we are particularly affirmed and gratified by a display of power and domination, especially in the male dancer. That is what "machismo" is all about. We find this exciting—living it up—but when this happens, it masks the deeper sense, that of existing, sheer aliveness.

Therefore, art that deprives us of this gift of aliveness leaves us in dead matter and lets us wallow in our suffering, in our hopes and fears, and is ultimately vulgar and trivial.

So you can see that in standing at the end of "pine tree," I was just presenting a metaphor in dance art.

When we use the formula "express yourself" in art, we really mean that we wish to reveal our personal hopes and fears, whether we are succeeding or failing in our pretention to be the big cheese, the only pebble on the beach, the center of the world.

I regret to say that once in the Western world, at the time of the Renaissance, we lost the perennial tradition of the purpose of making art. We fell into the trap of journalism, the idea that the task of the artist was to report. This reporting can be in the form of reporting actions in the social world, whereby you get realism, or in the form of inner reporting, "telling it LIKE it is" in the individual's success or failure, in an effort to win total, undeviating affirmation. Have you ever felt this kind of art had a deadness to it? And wondered why?

This idea about art, recent in the Western world, leads to wallowing in negativity, sentimentality, escapism, triviality, and ultimately, vulgarity: the reason being it is always dead.

Hence, ladies and gentlemen, I'm against it.

The distinction, which can be shown to make the point clear, is between living, in the sense we use in slang of "living it up"— violent upheavals and titillations of illusions, hopes and fears—and something else as an alternate, which is different enough, which is the "given," existing.

Now this is a big field for thinking, so here I don't imagine I can do more than adumbrate the notion and relate it to my intuition about the art of dance.

A good example of "living," or "living it up" which is an underlying notion to all the undeveloped souls of our society, was shockingly reported in the *New York Times* lately about a teenage brother and sister in Cleveland who gave money to another young man to kill their father because he wouldn't let them have any fun and wouldn't let them smoke pot.

This kind of idea as being valid for works of art—doing something for satisfying the ego, for having things your own way, for ruthlessness to others, animals or humans—has permeated our art far too much, even though it is concurrent with some glorious new art.

Where it often shows in dance art today is a desire on the part of the audience to see and experience psychological violence and negativity and expressions of egotism. Another manifestation is the desire for novelty, which easily leads to absurdity and a taste for bizarre perversion and exaggeration.

My call to order, *rappel à l'ordre*, surely appropriate for this time, is to ask those who are ready for it to understand the metaphysical position of eliminating the phantoms of the human mind, the restlessness of spirit, the ignorance of the relation of each ego to everything else in the world, and therefore, at the end, to arrive at an appreciation of just existing.

I would like to see a point of view of dance which can flow only from a philosophical notion that has been diligently looked at in each artist's, each spectator's, experience.

I present my intuition which you will have to receive as only that. What has been said up to now paves the way for something that can be formulated more explicitly.

The corollary of the sense of "existence" as contrasted with "life" is the difference of experiencing one's inner and outer world in the aesthetic dimension, rather than in the psychological dimension.

I suspect that when I make the contradistinction between art that more nearly stays in the aesthetic dimension, and art that battens in the psychological dimension, I will start to perplex many listeners who, up to now, have maintained rather exclusively the general tradition of Western art, certainly as it turned a corner at the time of the Renaissance, with its growth of emphasis on human individualism.

One of the character traits I have discovered—both in myself and as I watch my fellow travelers—that lets us grow, relax, develop a light touch, is the ability to recognize when we have made a mistake in point of view and switch fast to let a new insight plant its roots. Why, right in teaching dance technique to hundreds of young people as I do each year, there is a noticeable difference in character of those students who quickly recognize the teacher is telling them something more to the point, more complete, therefore more open to change and more movement, and those who can't bear to appear green or wrong.

Perhaps this is a time in the set of notions of Western art when we are ready to see that our way omitted some values that people in Asia and the Indians of North America right here have developed in a fruitful way.

Please don't confuse the point I am making with the actions of the ever increasing hordes of fashionmongers in the arts who, having nothing of their own vitality and inner experience to say, are doing Tibetan chants, African drumming, Whirling Dervishing, writing sutras, vulgar haiku and such.

No, I am referring to ideas that are implicit in Western art, but relatively undeveloped, just because there aren't enough artists ready to stick their necks out for certain ideas.

It is not a question of either/or. It is a question of proportion and applicability. The both/and position is most brilliantly and completely illuminated in *The Meeting of East and West,* by F.S.C. Northrop.

There is a great implication for a growth of wisdom in the human race in seeing the difference between a doctrine that can say, "If you meet the Buddha, kill him" and one that says, "Ours is the only God and if you don't bow down to him, off with your head."

It has taken me a long time of growing up to realize that everyone in the world is doing the best he can. I think no one would appreciate an elegant, efficient, loving society more than I, but I know now that nothing happens except through the change of consciousness of any individual.

So I propose that you look at this fact, that the West doesn't know everything and that it is wisdom to recognize what you don't know, if it has value for your civilization. When I am saying that the West, from the Renaissance on, has developed an excessive concern with individualism, I mean to suggest we check up on our ideas.

There is a real paradox here. Maybe I can illustrate it from observations I see daily in teaching technique. Actually, now that I think of it, this point, both in practice and theory, makes my teaching of technique slightly maverick.

Most people grow up without realizing that if they do their own thing when they walk down the street, they are deforming their bodies. They do not realize that individualistic movements that permit shifts of weight away from an ideal, physically determined axis or center of balance—a principle common to all—are perverse, eccentric, damaging. Beautiful movement can result only from the instinctive obedience to the physical laws of nature of the human body . . . just as it would be perverse to eat hay instead of what humans can digest, or to hit your thumb hard with a hammer three times a day, or to kick a baby every time it smiled at you.

The human mind thinks it can make the organism do anything it can imagine. That way is madness and self-destruction. If you think you can feed your body with drugs, you are mistaken. If you think I am far afield, I assure you I am not. What the artist does to make art and the spectator does to receive it, is in no way disconnected from what he, as artist or spectator, thinks about everything else in the world. I wish I knew some poet who bound all men and things together with the power Donne did: "Do not send to know for whom the bell tolls, It tolls for thee."

In America, there is still the feeling that art is something you can take or leave. But our sadness in the midst of plenty belies that idea.

What I mean by the psychological dimension in art, as contrasted with the aesthetic dimension, refers to an excessive concern with a less spiritually developed attitude toward human existence and means undue concern with the human ego, greediness for "living it up," dominating others, indulging in self-pity, fighting for a buck and, ultimately, to pandering.

In contrast, the aesthetic dimension in art is art that proposes the spectator's step outside his little ME concerns and in a more neutral, larger way, look at the wondrousness of the world and the mystery of being alive.

In a few words, one can say that a great deal of the best of Far Eastern art, like a Japanese stone garden, points to just looking at Things. The existence of Things, and the treasuring of them, leads the onlooker to forget himself and remember that he, too, is part of Nature, of these Things. In the mythology of the North American Indians, there is usually a demiurge, but never a God who created nature, separate from the creator. It makes a whole difference in society's attitude toward art and existence and nature.

I believe I can categorically say, with few exceptions, that all of the most beautiful dancing I have ever seen (and samples of every great dance culture have come to New York in my lifetime) have been non-Western.

It is because of their absence of emphasis on individualistic display of power and domination and pretensions to be separate from the rest of all created things, and therefore, insensitive.

When one stays in the aesthetic dimension in art and dance, one taps the greatest reservoir of human sensitivity. One can enjoy many elements of the sensuous materials of art, and slough off the vanity of triumph, the virtuosity which is the virtuosity of the circus, achievement of the measurable stunt, and essentially a psychological phenomenon.

The aesthetic dimension is something else. It is more transparent. It is closer to looking at the world and one's existence as the Southwest African bushmen do when they say the four most beautiful things in the world are lightning, thunder, a falling star and the roar of a lion.

A sensitive distinction I would like to throw out is that made by Jacques Maritain between art and poetry. The poetry of any art or anything in the outer world of things is something you see or you don't. You have heard that some people are color-blind. For example, their eyes don't see a green.

Well, I fear that some people have not awakened to the fact that this ineffable thing called "poetry," the source of wonder, exists and that to have it is the birthright of all.

I consider a high culture one in which the people experience their existence poetically, that is, with wonder. When one sees things wondrously, one is always grateful. When one is grateful, one is always full of love and tenderness toward oneself, others, the animals, and the very stones.

When one sees a work of art that is purely in the aesthetic dimension, there is no choice but to catch one's breath. One knows one is alive.

One of the great experiences of my life was coming, a few months ago, to the new East Wing of the National Gallery of Art in Washington, D.C., just a few streets away. I could not believe my eyes. How extraordinary that in this day and age, wise factors had achieved a building and gathering together of painting and sculpture of our time that were all completely and perfectly in the aesthetic dimension, and in no way presented psychological distortions.

I was overwhelmed by beauty—the Motherwells, the Calders, the Noguchis, the David Smiths—all artists whom I had known and loved, and even worked with. By the time I got to the turret at the top and the Matisses flooded my eyes, I burst into tears and had to sob.

When I finally had to leave, I knew that I was like some fellow citizen of Pericles who returned to Athens from a long voyage and saw the Parthenon all at once.

The extraordinary achievement was that the Pericles of our day had built such a triumph in purely the aesthetic dimension. There was no junk, no perversion, no psychological unwisdom or immaturity, no aggressiveness, no tricks, no virtuosity.

Virtuosity in dance—very slightly—borders on circus, as I have said. Real virtuosity is always at the service of the poetry of the work.

There is one aspect of my subject which could be misunderstood. I have written about this aspect elsewhere as in "The Body Is a Clear Place," but I would not like anyone to interpret what I have said up to now to mean that the aesthetic dimension in art excludes what we ordinarily mean by "representational," or having subject matter.

I refer you again to *The Meeting of East and West* in which Northrop clearly enunciates the prime notion in all aesthetic thinking.

In summary, he formulates two aspects of all art, art in its first function and art in its second function.

By art in its first function, he refers to art which uses its materials, colors, shapes, sounds, textures and movements in and for their own sake.

Art in its second function uses these elements to convey ideas of any kind in human experience which are not right there in the prime materials. It is using this luminous existence to express the wisdom of the race and embody this wisdom with aliveness. This is the sheer, the luminous, the existing.

These two functions are, somewhat, the two ends of a scale and so any work can lodge at a pointer reading between the two polar absolutes.

The opening exhibition of the East Wing was a thrilling and unique presentation and recapitulation of art that could be almost totally described by Northrop's definition of art in its first function.

Works of art that stay within the first function are closer to my meaning of metaphors of existence, because they denote nothing beyond themselves. And in that way can be a metaphor for existence which aims at nothing, and merely stands and says, "Thank you." This is the primal function of any art. Without this, there is no art. For me, dance has the chance to be the most primal of the arts.

The philosophy of "art in its first function" is the great revolution in modern times in the West, for it gave a new primacy to immediate experience. That is why modern art in general, apart from all the bad and erroneous art included in "modern art" as in "modern dance," has been harder for the general Western audience to "get."

In general, we in the West shy away from valuing immediate

experience, though I suspect that it is a human problem, not just a Western problem. Maybe that is why Buddhism needed to travel from India to China and join Taoism to make Zen Buddhism in China and Japan, and in my lifetime, travel to America. That whole odyssey was a passionate search for direct experience.

The self-cultivation of the immediacy of existing maybe, then, is a task for all cultures. It is a fact that Oriental and other non-Western philosophy more wholeheartedly put a premium on "radical empirical immediacy," as Northrop calls it.

Scottish philosopher David Hume was one of the first to point out that we do not experience the world around us directly or automatically, unless we know how. And therein lies our fate: in deadness or aliveness.

Works of art that remain primarily art in its first function are the only way to lead to the experience of immediacy, to our just existing.

Art in its second function has its own importance, which is different: to take the wisdom of the race, the ideas, the concepts, and express them in works of art, through sensuous materials. This wisdom is valuable, but unimmediate.

A scientist can grasp intellectually the whole cosmos, but in his scientific formulations, he cannot experience it directly. And so it always remains strangely unalive and alien to him.

The importance of art in its second function and its unique role is to take this valuable but non-immediate, unalive wisdom and bring it to surprising newborn life through the immediacy of the luminous materials of art in its first function. In this way, the scientist's universe becomes alive.

Actually, our society badly needs great works of art and great dancers to express metaphysical ideas with brilliance and power. Picasso's "Guernica" is a wonderful example. Even greater are the Navajo sand paintings.

A footnote is needed here. All works of art in its second function require a superb use of the materials that are the essence of art in its first function. We have to keep remembering to be alive.

An example in my own work of the contrast of art in its first function and art in its second function is "Here and Now With Watchers," which I referred to earlier. Of this evening-length work, the first six sections are entirely immediacy. This significance is what "Here and Now" in the title refers.

But the seventh and eighth dances, "clown is everyone's ending," and "like DARLING," the love duet, are art in its second functions, for they refer to ideas in the human mind and soul, not directly happening just on that stage at that time.

The dances in the two functions of art were structured into the large entity of this dance exactly to arrive at a totality of possibility.

Now that I have lived long enough to develop some skill, and understand a little of how art works, I wish I had another lifetime to make dances of power and completeness in the area of art in its second function.

It seems to be a great error, alarmingly compounded in the last two hundred years, that the young can be born and left on their own. On the contrary, the human species lives not through instinct, but through culture. Culture means the passing on of knowledge and sensibility from the experienced to the young.

One of the most obvious examples of how the young need to be taught is right in the movement of the body. Human beings have to be taught to use their bodies according to the exact reality of scientific laws of movement, that is, according to nature, the nature of things.

Religion has always been the effort of human societies to explain how the inner and outer worlds work. Because as mankind got to understand more, to be brighter, to see larger relationships, and so in time wanted to correct old, inadequate views, the appearance was to tear down religion. Hence, the standard dilemma in all societies today.

The trouble seems to be that we haven't succeeded, as yet, in clearly supplanting outworn religious ideas by new productive, more correct ones. Joseph Campbell, in his wonderful little book, *Myths to Live By*, points out the bathos of the first astronauts as they approached the moon landing, sending back to the audience— Earth—their sense of the wondrousness of their fantastic journey, by reading into the radio the words of the creation from the *Book of Genesis*, totally parochial and outworn.

I wish to make clear this very important point. The world is crying out for the artists to make works of art in the second function, that is, to convey ideas that derive from and are commensurate with the refined and distilled wisdom of the thinking leaders of our contemporary society.

It is for this reason that artists must be wise and complete men and women, so they will be ready to convey mature wisdom to audiences.

The image of the artist as a freak, an egotistic self-exposer, an exhibitionist, reveals a degraded culture. That is why, too, an artist, when he is concerned with conveying metaphysical ideas by which mankind lives, cannot be concerned only with the truth of what he has to convey.

I have always longed for a time when choreographers would have the courage to tackle themes that were really complete, really religious, that were really rituals of the journey of the soul. Please understand, by that I do not mean long works that report. I mean works that convey events in the inner psychic life, where the hero conquers the monsters.

In 1952, on a small scale, I tried a series of five solos called "openings of the (eye)." They were a progression of metaphors of states of metaphysical knowledge. The metaphors were clothed in striking images in the design of sets and costumes by Ralph Dorazio. Lucia Dlugoszewski wrote a unique score of it. But I was too far ahead of my time, and few people were aware of the metaphors and how to read them.

Beautiful and strong dances as art in its second function, were they achieved, could become beautiful rituals—rituals by which the audience recollected periodically what it knew, what it understood of the world and existence.

But in the earlier part of this essay, in speaking about dances made in the first function of art, and about most of the painting and sculpture in the new East Wing, I was proposing an emphasis on works of art that had nothing to do with our understanding of our world, even our inner psychic world, but with merely sensing our existence.

At the moment when we are just sensing our existence, we are not even concerned with whether or not we are hungry, or whether we understand anything. We are just here, now.

From everything I can pick up of the wisest writing from all times and places, the really bright writers are pointing just to the mystery of being alive.

When you try to make an equivalent of this in art, then you enter the aesthetic dimension, as I said above. It is perhaps true that to make a dance which stays clearly in the aesthetic dimension requires a pinpointed innocence, which is not easy to arrive at. Hence, by definition, it is the pearl of great price. For an audience too, to come to a dance in the aesthetic dimension requires innocence, a keen inner development by which egotistical grubbiness and pettiness is abandoned. Watching dances like these means accepting the invitation to a ceremony of awareness.

Dances remaining in the aesthetic dimension transcend "doing" and point out "being," a hard thing for many Western audiences.

If you want to read some beautiful sentences about this, look up essays about the Southwest Indians by D. H. Lawrence in his *Mornings in Mexico*.

Dance as a Metaphor of Existence.

Dance more than any other art or any activity is the metaphor par excellence, and that is why I am so thrilled and moved by it, because the very ground of dance is the complete entity of body and mind, heightened in its doing, in time.

The body moves and it stops, and it will never happen again. Our strange, unfathomable, ineffable existence.

Nine/ The Principle of a Thing

This essay was written for this collection, 1991.

The *principle* of a thing is how it works, how it organizes—the Latin word simply means *first* or *primary.* We speak in conversation of moral principles, of psychological principles, of physical principles. It is only when one understands the principle of a thing that one can determine the results. Without understanding the principle of a thing, one has no control, one cannot manipulate it to get a desired result.

One of the clearest explanations of what a physical principle is comes from the time of the Civil War. Some shipbuilders proposed to build ships of iron. But others said, "Don't you know that if you put a piece of iron in the water, it will sink. All the world knows that." But some shipbuilders on both sides knew that that was not the principle, and so they inaugurated a new method of building ships. The South used large plates of iron to cover their old wooden ships, while the North used another procedure to build the *Monitor,* made totally of iron, which was close to the water. The principle was *not* that iron, when put into water, will sink, or that a piece of wood, put into water, being light, floats. In other words, it has nothing to do with the weight of the floating object. But the true principle is that the amount of volume of the water that the object displaces can be either lighter or heavier than the object, so that a piece of iron, not displacing much water, will sink, while a piece of wood, being lighter than the water it displaces, will float.

Go back to childhood when you had frogs and fishes of celluloid and plastic that floated in your tub, while heavier things like most ordinary soaps sank to the bottom.

In ordinary experience even a child will sense an object like iron will sink or an object like wood will float. But shipbuilders at the time of the Civil War needed to be cognizant of the principle of why a celluloid fish floats or some soap sinks. In that way they could enlarge on the principle and make ships of iron such as our modern Navy does today.

When the United States gave tractors to nations in southeast Asia, the tractors ran as long as they did not need repairs. When the Asians did not understand the principle of the machine, how it was built, and how it worked . . . when left to their own, the machines stood idle, or the Asians attempted to repair them with string or other totally inadequate material.

The principle of a thing is quite abstract to ordinary common sense. In general, it is not seen by the ordinary observer or by one's own senses.

Sometimes the principle of a thing can be called "the theory" of a thing.

To understand "the theory" of a procedure is to understand its "principle."

Sometimes one hears it said, "Oh, that's theoretical." But people who say that forget that everything we do depends upon a theory. In any activity the practice can only come out of "a theory." Some image in the mind has to direct the action. It may be an unconscious image or an idea, but that is the way the mind works. If women cannot drive automobiles in Saudi Arabia, that comes from a "theory"—the "theory" that women are not the equivalent of men.

The fact that men can land on the moon is a direct result of the building up of knowledge in physics to achieve that result. That is why philosophy is merely looking at your basic premises. That is why the training for dance, the movement, and finally the choreography, hinges on "philosophy."

Once I heard a dancer speaking at Cooper Union during the question and answer period; a man off the street asked, "Mister—, what was your philosophy in the dance you just did?" The dancer answered, "I have no philosophy." But to have no philosophy is to have a philosophy.

This essay is to put my thoughts briefly down for a new philosophy about dance training.

First, the whim of the individual dancer is not the criterion. On this first level, no movement that the individual dancer likes and often uses is basic enough. The only way a dance training can be valid is when it is based on scientific knowledge, not on personal whims or eccentricities. That can, perhaps, come later, when one's individual vocabulary is established. But the principle that I'm talking about is prior to the individual's vocabulary. What is known in science is known by all knowers. That is what science means. Any dance student, since the human organism is all one, needs to be aware consciously or unconsciously of the scientific basis for movement, since every human being in the world has the same physical requirements of how to move. If you know the scientific knowledge of the human body, whether you live in Asia, America, Africa, or wherever, you will not make mistakes in your movement that will cause injury or limitation. You will obey the principle of movement regardless of where you live; you will understand "how the body works." How the body works is to have no limitation but freedom.

One of the tasks of a dance teacher is to show the student how not to carry along limitations of the past that he has picked up from parents, teachers, and playmates.[32] That is why a dance teacher has to have real experience in knowing what errors the human body can acquire in growing up because he has to eliminate all the actions that are limiting the student.

The dance student doesn't have to know about kinesiology per se, but the dance teacher has to incorporate the truths into the exposition of technique. Of course, if the dance student has a clear image of the general way the body works—its bones, joints, and muscles—those images can very much help maintain the correct perfection of good body-management. Anything the dance student can do to visualize the inner action of the body with vividness is a great help. When dancing, one doesn't visualize what the body is doing all the time, but at flickering moments the sensation of the body can be vivified, and brought to life, and that makes vivid dancing.

In cultures of dance training that do not have a scientific knowledge of kinesiology, the task is to hang onto their original perception of how the body moves. We in the West have to increase our knowledge since, in general, we have lost the instinctive intuition of how the body moves. Science is made up of a lot of observable data before the theory is formulated. We in the West need a scientific knowledge of movement; other cultures need to preserve their intuitive and long built-up experience of the body.

This intuitive knowledge of the body and how it moves can easily be lost. In the third century B.C., the Greek scientist Eratosthenes measured the diameter of the earth within a few hundred miles of what it actually is, without any instruments such as we have now, but the knowledge of this was lost. We are here in America because Christopher Columbus thought that the world was round and tried to prove it. But somebody already knew it.

It seems to me that at the height of Greek culture, around 400 B.C., the understanding of the beautiful body was quite prevalent. But it too was lost in the course of time. It is to the glory of an American, Isadora Duncan, that today in dancing we in the West have an image of the natural human body and its movement. Of course, there were other people in the Renaissance, namely the painters, who showed evidence that they understood, but this intuitive, natural action of the body was distorted for theological reasons, and for the development of art leading to the ballet which had its antecedents in the customs of the court. The revolution that Isadora Duncan foresaw has only partly happened.

The present-day training of dance in America, as in Europe too, is rather mixed-up. Isadora Duncan's vision about dancing went back to the Greek idea that the body is beautiful, and made a link to a new consciousness in the modern world that the dance is the prime experience of the human race, tied in with all of the new enlargements of the consciousness of modern man.

But the revolution she foresaw has not yet happened in dance training, much less in the vocabulary. The modern dance used certain of the insights of Isadora Duncan in finding the freedom of the infinite possibilities dance has.

But the main principle of her understanding has not surfaced very extensively. That is what this essay is about. The main aspect is adumbrated in a distinction that Rudolf Von Laban and Irmgard Bartenieff arrived at in speaking of movement as having *bound flow* and *free flow*. What I write may not be exactly what Bartenieff meant, but it does give an indication between bound flow and free flow, which is the heart of the matter.

It was some years ago that Miss Bartenieff called Martha Graham's technique bound flow, and my insights into what we should strive for as free flow.

It seems obvious to me that, by definition, free flow is ever moving, ever active, quick shifts of weight, joyous, an unleashed spirit that is life-giving and is right. Only when muscles are free flowing do they shift weight and work fast enough to accomplish a "speedy" movement. Who would want to be bound by a technique that had limitations in it, even when this is "codified"?

The main knowledge that comes out of the study of kinesiology is life-giving and integrates the minds and the body with this precept: When you make an action, just do the movement.

It means that no willfulness from the mental image that the mind has (every movement comes out of a mental image) interferes with just doing the movement. When one understands the scientific reasoning behind kinesiology, one arrives at such unity of the body and mind that one simply "does the movement." The question is not to interfere with the movement by tightening the muscles erroneously in order to do the movement. Bound flow is trying to drive the car with the brakes on.

We are so used in the dance to showing willfulness and strain that the audience's evaluation is distorted.

A good example in common parlance is the saying, "No pain, no gain." This erroneous notion that has gone into dance training ties people up in knots (literally, knots). My saying over the years is "Tight muscles cannot feel." Only muscles that act harmoniously and without strain are therefore efficient and ready for the next movement.

In Hubert Benoit's *The Supreme Doctrine*, I picked up a word which I have almost never seen in any other context for what I am talking about. That word is "coenesthesia" (coen = common; esthesia = feeling). So the word means, in Greek, a commonly felt state of sensation, how much contraction or decontraction there is in the body. The body needs to flicker in the stronger contraction and decontraction depending upon what the mind says the action is to be. This is very hard to talk about.

It is only when the consciousness goes into the body's experience that one can see the difference from the outside. One day when I was fixing up my first studio on 17th Street, a young man who had been in the war came to help me. It was a Sunday afternoon. All at once I looked at him and he came to a full catatonic state; he stood upright like a rigid board, and then fell to the floor. I don't know how he didn't break his nose, or maybe he did, but I had to call Bellevue Hospital for an ambulance. This example shows that the body can tighten all of the muscles so directly that one feels like a board with no life, and no movement.

I had the opposite experience where the consciousness went out of the organism, when I was giving blood and must have been in bad shape, because, ordinarily, I don't faint very often. But in this case I fainted, fell to the floor, the blood spilled on the nurse's stockings, and I lost all sensation of holding myself up.

These are two extremes of contraction and decontraction.

You might say that the contraction was on one end of the scale where it was total contraction, and the way I fainted was decontraction at the opposite end of the scale.

Every person, and therefore every dance student, is always in between the catatonic state and fainting. Every person and every dance student needs to find the correct place on the scale to do what is needed to be done. The brain tells one the movement that one wants to do. The image in the brain decides whether it's a movement of contraction or decontraction.

The dancer has to feel what action he wants to do, and not interfere with it.

If the theory is incorrect, then the dance student is misled as to how much effort to apply to the movement on the scale between contraction and decontraction.

Nothing is ever separated from any other relationship in the world. When one speaks of the correct amount of contraction and decontraction to do a certain movement, one is led to make similar analogies. When you open a drawer and the friction doesn't quite permit the drawer to open easily, the strain[33] is analogous to the body not having easiness of action. The further analogy is a spiritual one.

The recurring endeavor is finding how mental imagery affects the physical world. It soon became evident to me that strain in the body asked for strain in the soul or psyche, or whatever we call the inward man. As I grew up I saw evidences that spiritual enlightenment, or whatever else you want to call it, has its analogy in the grace of the body. The goal is to avoid strain on any level of activity: mental or physical, personal or political, and cultural. The goal of all spiritual leaders is to avoid strain. They want harmony in all kinds of moral and physical areas.

The famous statue of the dance of Shiva has one of its arms in a mudras sign language, saying, "Fear not." The Buddhist teaching is again, "Do not Fear." If you look up to the North Pole, the Eskimo shaman says, "Be not afraid of the Universe." The most up-to-date psychological teaching is, if you want the living organism to flower, it will blossom through love and not being afraid.

It seems to me that what you might call the mental world or the spiritual world has an exact analogy in the training of the body so the body will do what is needed without strain.

In my early years and even today, I run into pupils and even older dance teachers who apologize that they can't do a certain range of movements because they have hurt their knees. What that hurt could have been varies with each person. But the very fact that the dance can be taught and accepted when it might injure the knee shows how erroneous the knowledge of the body is, in general.

It seems a great pity that older dancers who should have long experience to produce beautiful art should be thrown on the ash heap before their time. My saying is that an injury is an ignorance. It means that the learning of the dancer has not been grounded in correct knowledge of how the body works, and so an injury is doing something that is against nature. One of our most famous ballerinas lately had the thigh sockets of both hips replaced, which means, of course, that she stopped dancing. Something is wrong when the technical demands tear down the harmonious ease of the body. As in times past, a high range in the male voice as in Gluck's *Orpheus* was done by castrating the men, just as in China, a woman's feet were bound to embody an ideal of the social status of a woman. It's too great a price to pay in terms of human happiness.

The individual movements that the dancer makes according to his native intuition, when he forgets the implications of the theory, are correct. The ballet dancer drops what he has been taught by theory and permits himself by intuition to move according to nature. The theory always gets in the way, and that's what I'm talking about. The theory is to do movements with bound flow—that is, tightening the muscles in order to do the movement. Likewise the teaching of the Martha Graham School in doing the equivalent of bound flow is in error. Tightening the muscles before you do the movement is always an error. Just as in Dr. Bates' method of sight without glasses, strain is an error because it limits eyesight.

One of our great American poets, e.e. cummings, renders this idea beautifully: "Doubting turns men's see to stare." Staring means fixating and that's why tight muscles cannot feel. When muscles can contract and decontract like the eyes, then they are achieving their fullness of use.

Of course, it is true that human beings utilize their own intuitive sense of how to use the body rightly. In individual movements, a ballet dancer will do things according to nature, that is, rightly.

But here is where the idea of theory comes into the picture. If one's action is to squeeze the muscles in order to do a movement, then I am reminded of one of my first teachers at the School of American Ballet. Even then, I did not know why, but I knew something was wrong with the way she held her shoulders and ribs. She denied the grace and loveliness of her own natural movement.

Recently on our Asian tour to Japan and China, I gave a lesson at the Shanghai Ballet School. After the class, one of the young men showed me some pictures of himself. I recall he had won some international competition; in those pictures, I could see the theory of ballet in practice. The young Chinese man had picked up all of the erroneous stances from the Soviet Russian ballet and was priding himself on the correctness of his picture. Not only was his technique wrong, but the vocabulary was so unmanly, whether Chinese or Russian or American. The young man was not unmanly but his vocabulary was unmanly. The theory had been transferred to China just as it had been transferred to America.

That is what I am talking about. If the theory is incorrect, you'll get practices that are incorrect. The correct theory can only be in accordance with nature, in this case, scientific observation of how the body works.

One of the main points that enters into a discussion on ballet and the general run of modern dance is that the body is the same body. It's not that every movement in ballet is wrong, or that any movement in so-called modern dance is right. Modern dance people can be as egregiously wrong in doing a movement as their so-called ballet brethren. The point is that any movement in any vocabulary, or tradition, can be right or wrong depending on whether the physical basis is according to nature, "according to nature" being based on scientific observation and theory.

If a plié in second is done in ballet with the correct idea, it's far more useful than the movement done incorrectly in a modern dance context.

Many people think that ultimately there is no difference between ballet and modern dance. Martha Graham, in a famous statement, said, "I do not see any difference between ballet and modern. I see only good dancing and bad dancing." That obscures the issue.

There is a difference in vocabulary but also in whether the scientific principle is right for a new, enlightened dance or for an old dance. It seems to me that this was Martha's turning her back on everything that she originally stood for. This is one of the places where technique and vocabulary are mixed up.

Of course, Martha, in something like *Primitive Mysteries,* was forging new ground, and it was a glorious one. But she was unaware of the point I am making and that is what is called the principle of a thing.

It is very easy to get confused. The correct scientific principle is confounded very much with an aesthetic vocabulary. I can perhaps be a little autobiographical. After four years of studying under Balanchine, after being in his first American dance called *Serenade,* and after being the first beginning student to teach beginning classes, soon I found out that the St. Petersburg "Geist" did not fit well with the fact that I was brought up in the Western Plains at the base of the Rockies. The general notion of a man's dancing in the ballet tradition made me think I would never arrive at my own sense of being. That was a large part of the burgeoning attempt to make a modern dance. The vocabulary was incomplete. By that time it was very restricted in movement and feeling. One of the reasons that Balanchine intrigued me so, and I accepted him as a teacher, was because he was trying within the framework of ballet to make new poetic excursions.

So, of course, many people like Martha or myself in turn wanted a new enlargement in the field of movement.

But here, leaving aside the vocabulary, one returns to technique. It is the technique, the know-how, that is the main point at issue.

I run into student after student like the young student at the Shanghai Ballet who prided himself on what he'd picked up from the Russian Ballet, who has been taught wrongly how to think-feel in the body. It is on the scale of contraction-decontraction that one has to find the rightness according to the movement one chooses to do, without interfering in the mind or in the musculature to avoid errors. So there are two levels in which a well-grounded modern dance can be built up.

The first is getting the scientific basis for correct movement as a starting point. The second is feeling that the codification of ballet movement is too restricted. And that is why every good original in modern dance like Doris Humphrey or Martha Graham or many of us in the second generation have contributed a wonderful range of movement.

I have often wondered just how history will put it into words; will ballet absorb the modern dance or will modern dance assimilate and absorb ballet?

I think it is the second of these choices. Modern dance cannot be confined to those terms. It is a wide vision of human movement. In general, the larger principle can include the smaller principle.

When I am confronted with a student who wants to know his way in the confusion of whether he should have ballet training or modern dance training, I'm always tempted to say that if you learn the right principle of movement, then you'll be able to do anything. So if a modern dancer arrives at a correct scientific way of experiencing the movement, he can do everything possible that human movement can do, turns in second, double air turns, all kinds of movements that quickly become stunts.

I remember the first time, in Martha's *Deaths and Entrances,* when I, in finding the choreography for my own part, used a double air turn. It was not art in its first function but art in its second function. I was quite aware that I was doing it out of the emotional explosion—the way the piece was going.

The choreographer, to be a valid and worthy artist, would have to make up new vocabulary.

At the time the modern dance began to exist in America, balletic choreography was at a dead end.

It is possible to codify the movement vocabulary with such stringent rules that you still call it balletic, but it is utterly dull, and has no adventure. That is always the problem of codifying anything. You rule out new possibilities.

Years ago when my company performed at Jacob's Pillow, Xemenez and Vargas were on the same program. Xemenez and Vargas used to hover around Lucia Dlugoszewski offstage as they watched the new music and the new dancing done. I had the feeling from conversation that they wanted to enlarge their vocabulary. Of course, they didn't come, and in one sense, it would have served no purpose for their coming. The point is, they were tied into old vocabulary no matter how glorious the Spanish dance is. So today the dilemma is not to have too rigid a codification unless one will pay the price of restricting the vocabulary of the student.

It is a constant dilemma to me, in running my school, whether I suggest that the numerous teachers follow those leads that I have of what I find prepares the body for a class, whether I hold them to that, or whether I let the teachers make up their own movements. I have decided on the possibility of freedom.

That is what I mean by understanding the principle of a thing. If the teachers make up their own movements (and I'm amazed and delighted with what they do), I know that they are doing it because they understand the principle I have taught them. If you do any movement by understanding the principle it will not be wrong. (Of course, the teacher can use bad judgment in trying something too hard for what the student can do, but it will not violate the principle.)

I am sure it is going to take a long time before the understanding is complete in something called the modern dance. When the correct foundation for a scientifically based dance training is generally understood, then the modern dance can flower without error, and make a glorious era.

Ballet is a definite set of movements done in a certain way, passing from Italy to France to Russia and to America, with a certain range of movements as a backlog of their dance training. The human body has only two feet, just as in music, our formulation is in an octave with eight tones. But within that octave you can make billions of movements, and that is why the modern dance is unlimited in its possibilities.

I remember once saying to Robert Motherwell after seeing an exhibition, "Motherwell, it is amazing to me how you make new shapes; it is as though you carve them from the 'uncarved block' as ancient Chinese artists say." What we want to see is how one brings up movement from the "uncarved block" (it is not gimmickry or attention-getting contradictoriness nor kookiness).

One of the prime errors in ballet training as I have seen it is the use of the pelvis and the lower back. One of the reasons that photographs of ballet dancers look stiff and unyielding is that the muscles in the lower back are held tightly. In the past I have asked, while on tour in America, what was the general teaching of ballet schools. If I asked, "Where is the center of the body and where does one have the most strength?" the clichéd response by dance students was that they were taught that the lower back was the center, and was where they had their main strength. That was typical of the Shanghai ballet student and that thinking is in error. The center is in the front, in the muscles that knit the body together, like the psoas, and give one control over the leg movement.

In working my very early duet on my own, I made a movement that I had to pay for not only by agonizing hours of being limited, but also by doctor bills. Because of the injury, I began to learn something about kinesiology, but not only kinesiology; it was finding my awareness in my own body.

Martha Graham, in her teaching, did not know what to tell me to do. This is why one needs a theory, not just a personal whim. The teacher needs to be able to tell a student, if he sees any tightness in the lower back, how to lengthen it by visualization.

Many movements in ballet technique lead one to this error. How you do the movement avoids this error. Sensing oneself in the scale of contraction and decontraction through practice you can avoid this error.

Sometime after I was working on my own, I was asked in Portland, Oregon, "Where do you think the center of the body is?" I thought it over to myself as I was waiting to have my hostess pay the check, and I realized where I really felt it. It was in front of the pelvis. Later on, a lawyer friend of mine said, "Erick, have you ever heard of Aikido?" When I answered no, he said, "I'll send you a little book about it." Imagine my surprise when I found it was long-time known in Aikido that the center of the body was in the front of the pelvis.

People have said that I was influenced in general in technique and vocabulary or aesthetics by the Orient. I finally arrived at the same principle that makes their arts. The principle of the center of the body being in the front below the navel confirmed what I was beginning to find out. That clinched it for me, that the main theory of ballet was incorrect. Especially now that I can relieve strain in dance students by having them feel an elongation rather than a contraction in the lower back. This frees the body up totally and I do many exercises demonstrating how one can get the action around the thigh socket in bending forward. Now one is not limited by tightness in the lower back.[34] Therefore, I say, let's go on to build a new dance technique abandoning the errors of the old.

I think it is important to realize that there is only one truth—and that is how the body works. That is why a scientific knowledge of the body, namely kinesiology, is studied. On the vocabulary level there are a million choreographers. On the technique level there is only one truth. There is no personal whim on this level—the basic level—of how the body should move. In other words, the teacher needs to inform the student how one moves with ease and efficiency: Efficiency = Ease.

Rather than force the movement into a step beyond what it has been used to, the teacher needs to "coax" the dancer's body to edge along a little bit more than the student has done the previous day. This cannot be done by will on the teacher's part, or that of the student's, but only through imaging and imagination of a further activity beyond what was done the day before. I used the word "coax" meaning that by mental suggestion through enlarging the mind's possibility of doing more movement the student can achieve it. The image in the mind affects the lengthening of the muscle. (This is why there can be no strife or willfulness or anxiety in the classroom.) Each student is doing the best he can. If he could do more, he would. Every student wants to live life to the fullest. The teacher's job is to encourage a beginning student to do more movement than he ever thought possible. If a teacher brings his own troubles to the classroom, it would behoove him to leave the classroom. Each student has a tender soul and the teacher's job is to foster that soul with the end in view that the pupil can do more movement than he'd ever done before. Even when the student has no "talent" and is a slow learner, or has little equipment from the past to engage in dancing, once the student has been accepted as a pupil, it tears down the whole world when the teacher belittles the student and undermines his self-confidence. I inject this because I have seen evidence that the opposite is true.

It is because of the "coenesthesia" which is affected by mental anxiety that there should be only joyfulness and lovingness in the classroom. Otherwise the student's anxiety either to please himself or the teacher will result in an erroneous placement on the scale of contraction and decontraction which I mentioned before, and if that is incorrect and not placed on the scale of "coenesthesia" correctly, then movement is inefficient. Only efficient movement works well. Only efficient movement functions without limitation.

If you don't sweat hard to achieve a movement, how do you get strong? I am reminded of this idea when I go up to the Athletic Club and see most of the men work up a sweat by overdoing an action. This is no more necessary than a violinist or pianist working up a sweat to make his muscles move. Instead, doing the movement many times with the maximum efficiency alone builds strength. Efficient movement builds strength. That is why in a class the teacher uses his judgment to determine how many times a certain movement can be done.

A few years ago I was in a position where I could have some diving lessons. It had been in my early years of dance training that I did my last somersault. As I watched the swimming instructor teach some young boys I was aware that they always did the movement in the mind. This correct placement of the muscle action through imagery eliminates extra tension and the wrong placement on the scale of contraction—decontraction. What the diving student learns by the process of doing it in the mind is ease.

All movement that is efficient we designate as graceful. When I see somebody before me as I walk down the street, I can determine if he is using his body with grace. Ungracefulness means excentered-ness; one is moving the trunk in an excentered way.[35] It breaks my heart when I see a young woman or man wishing to be so "with it" or to have arrived at their full sexual attractiveness and see them, through ignorance, make excentered movements that destroy the efficiency of the movement.

Several times so-called critics have judged the dancers of my company as being "too graceful." How can you be too graceful? How can you obey the laws of movement too much? It's like choosing a high-priced motorcar and being content with some sluggish valves in the engine.

One might question how to find this correct placement on the scale of contraction and decontraction for any given movement. The answer is a kind of feeling introspected in the body and leads one into doing the correct effort for any movement. The kinesiological rule is to just do the movement. If the movement is a slash you can't bind the movement or grip the muscles to make the slash. Or if the movement is to pat someone on the behind, you don't have to grip the muscles in order to do the movement. The tenderness in the mind takes care of the movement in the action.

Some years ago there was a series of photographs of Balanchine playing with a cat. It seems that Balanchine did not derive an important lesson from playing with the cat. It appears that he did not make the transference from a cat's action to what I'm talking about as a correct way for moving the human body. The cat, when it struck out to claw an arm, or an object, was so instinctive and so natural that he did what you might call a kind of reflex. The human dancer always needs to do the movement by a kind of reflex, so to speak. The cat knows it by nature; the human student might need to learn this through practice until it becomes second nature to him. This is where the theory comes in. (All you can do is put your theory into practice. The student needs to know what action is needed to do it.) This makes for a great smoothness and grace, even when the cat's action has a kind of violence, or what may appear to be violence, in reacting to what it was doing.

In other words, the cat obeyed the laws of movement according to scientific kinesiology; he just did the movement. Can anyone say that the cat was too graceful?

The point of this essay is primarily to get the human dancer just to do the movement without any interference by a mistaken notion of tinkering with the muscles, such as tightening the buttocks in a plié in second, or any number of mistaken notions that the teacher might give to the student, trying to make the movement happen.

One of the reasons we are not accustomed as a culture to graceful movement is because we do not treasure it.

The saying among the Greeks of the Athenian supremacy was that the body was treasured and great sensitivity was used in the observation of the movement. They treasured the body by having many statues of Deity. Maybe they understood that the Gods are in the heart of man, and they understood that the body is a clear place.

That is why every nation in the working world would give its eye teeth to find a good example of the Greek sculpture of the time for its museum. By contrast, we today, only in spare moments, treasure the grace of an athlete or the grace of a woman. Our notion is mistakenly one of brute strength. We in our society do not treasure a truly graceful man or woman because we have perversions of what we think our manliness or womanliness is.

We do pay attention in the Olympics to the divers, swimmers, and ice skaters because they can move efficiently in what they do. At this point athletics is athletics and dance art should be dance art. The one thing that athletes and dancers have in common is that the means are through the body in its action. The dance art needs to be as efficient in scientific movement as athletics. The athletics are based primarily on quantitative measurement, how far can one run or win against competitors, how high can one jump in the high jump, how fast can one swim.

And it is here that dance in its one aspect is like athletics. I am reminded of that often by Jacques Maritain "in the creative intuition" in art and poetry. He says, "Virtuosity is an escape for the artist."

What he means is, beyond a certain point, if the dancer uses his body as a kind of stunt like so many pirouettes or so many double air turns, he is forgetting about his main job which is the poetry of dance. (At the same time you have to couple this saying of Maritain with an observation of Stanislavski, "The more talent you have, the more technique you need.")

In other words, one needs the technique in order to be able to do a wider range of movement efficiently. So the dance student must arrive through many repetitions of practice with maximum ease and grace. But his ease and grace in general, in dance, is at the service of poetry.

That is the difference between sport and art: the dance art primarily is to be at the service of poetry. (When I say poetry, it means the poetry of any art. This poetry is very difficult to talk about. I sometimes think people have it or don't have it.) It is seeing the world in its wondrousness in the light of, you might say, eternity. At this point anyone would have to visualize what is meant by "poetry." One of the ways that a teacher can convey this to a student is by doing the movement himself with the student copying him the best he can. But there is another way of using images. The mind will react to whatever suggestion it picks up from the outside world.

The mind has an image, or idea, from something seen in nature, or from a parent or a teacher. Only correct, life-giving ideas are going to pay off. Insofar as a teacher gives an incorrect idea to a pupil, one has an incorrect idea demonstrated by the pupil. This goes back to the point I made before, when I had my diving lessons and the teacher had taken time to let the student have a complete image of the dive before he did it. This can be used in dancing in one thousand different ways. The teacher can do the movement himself; that is the way Balinese dancers learn. Or the teacher can suggest an image in the mind of the correct form for the body and by keeping this correct form in the body as the movement is done, the student finally accomplishes it. It is here that either consciously or unconsciously the student needs to learn about the body through kinesiology. This is learning from the inside, not from the outside. The training of teachers doesn't have to be by the study of kinesiology per se, but the correct information needs to be part and parcel of the material that the teacher teaches. The training of teachers is that they have to have done the dancing before they can teach it. This can't be done from the outside. Only when you know what the coenesthesia is are you able to teach it. Now coenesthesia can be second nature and that's why the "good guys have it." But in general, most people who wish to be dancers have to learn and it can be taught. Sometimes I've seen people who have a correct coenesthesia turn out not to be interested in the dance as they grow up. I had one child in her early teens who was a marvelous instrument but she wanted to be an art teacher. Sometimes those who don't have native equipment for understanding can learn it so well that they can become masters.

I realized that this correct doctrine goes against many people's ideas of what dancing should be like and what the dance student training should be. It is so ingrained in our society, for all of Christianity's preaching the opposite, that to have exciting art you must have "Sturm und Drang," Storm and Strife. Christianity is trying to teach the opposite. We think that we have to have a tiger killing an antelope before we can see his beauty. We can't see the wondrousness of the tiger just to see his grace, his speed, his agility, just for his own liveliness and his being alive. In the same way, some critics think that my choreography is sleepy and that nothing happens. The refinement of subtle rhythms of inventive movement, the wonderful structure of the dancing, are lost on them. They have to see dancing that kicks up a storm to be happy.

The idea of decontracting at the right time in dance seems sleepy. It is not known to critics of dance who want all volume fortissimo. I am saying for the body to work best, it must decontract and therefore, at that moment, have lovelier movement. But that doesn't mean that the dancer can't make great bursts of energy without hecticness. Or perform action that is out of the framework of art.

Good art requires a certain tranquility, a dancer's looking at the action as he's doing it. I am reminded that when I was first in New York, Shankar gave a number of performances here. I remember counting them up; I went to see twenty-three performances. For the last performance, I either could have dinner or go to the performance. I chose the performance. I went, those days, when you could stand in a Broadway theater for $1.10. But I was so intrigued by the Indian dancing. When Indra was fighting the evil beings he did it all in dance and with a relaxed unhectic tranquility. But even more wonderful than Shankar was Shanta Rao. I think it was the most beautiful dancing I'd ever seen, or almost. One night in sheer ecstasy at the glory of her dancing and the music of the tabla and the sitar, forgetting myself, I called out, "How beautiful!"

The quick shifts of weight that make their rhythmic flow cannot be done by tight muscles.

It is a total misconception that what I am advocating from dance training cannot be used for strong attack and slashing movement and speed. In fact, it would further these qualities. This is the reasoning behind a correct theory for modern dance . . . not only for modern dance but for dance in general. Again, there's only one truth.

When I say there's only one truth, it means knowledge gained from everyone who looks at the material with science, and they can agree.

There is no personal whim. That is why this essay is an attempt to investigate what is correct theory behind dance training. The first step is knowing how the body works.

After that first knowledge about how the body works, then different cultures will find a multiplicity of vocabulary.

One of the errors in thinking "technique" in modern dance or balletic terms in the West is to confuse technique and vocabulary. Technique means how the body works.

Vocabulary is the means by which the movement is conveyed to the audience. In general, in modern dance and balletic terms in America, we confuse the two. The complete training for a dancer is to let him have such freedom in the body, such free flow, that he can do any kind of movement.

Vocabulary is the means by which the movement is chosen to express its meaning. The Spanish have a limited set of vocabulary. The Southwest Indians have a limited set of vocabulary. The Noh drama in Japan has a limited vocabulary. The African men from Cameroon whom I saw in 1964 in Paris have another limited set of vocabulary.

Each nation or particular location would choose to use a certain vocabulary, and it would be too bad to wipe this out by world-wide intercommunication.

Then comes the idea that individual artists would produce work based on their own liking. I may walk down the street, and out of a window, hear three or four bars of Mozart's vocabulary. He uses the same octave and instruments as everyone else in Western music, but I know by the way he puts notes together, their sequence, that it's Mozart. Any individual artist—for example, Gauguin—I don't have to know that it's Gauguin. When I see the picture, I see his vocabulary—it's Gauguin.

So, likewise in the art of dance, the way a choreographer likes certain sequences of movement, certain timings, and certain arrangements, spells out his individuality. This individuality is never to be confused with a "newness" in dance. That is, the newness aspect of dance is its great degradation. The newness of the last thirty years is not what I'm talking about. That is for pseudo-artists. The true artist loves certain sequences and tones and movements and takes delight in them so they're apt to show through in every dance. What one is always looking for is a new voice in music, in painting, in poetry, or in dance. But to be called a worthy art, the new work must fulfill a high excellence of all art that goes back to the Egyptians.

So one of the dangers is to confuse technique and vocabulary. For example, a person can have a very good vocabulary but have errors in technique, and, likewise, a person could have a good technique and turn out a very dull dance.

To find a complete art of dance we need the technique *AND* the vocabulary.

In another essay in this book I go into what Northrop calls "Art in its Second Function." When you are using vocabulary you can use art in its first function (when the emphasis is just on the handling of your art in painting, poetry, dance, music). Another aspect of art (which is very little understood) is "Art in its Second Function" where you use material of dance art, not only the use of rhythm or dynamics for their own sake but to express something, some idea, that is not on stage itself.

At this point, in speaking vocabulary, there are two directions—either a life-giving mode or a degenerate mode which tears down human life.

Vocabulary is a neutral term. In the essay "Art in its Second Function," I go into the possibility of life-giving or destructive aspects. But now let's leave vocabulary simply as the movements by which the idea is conveyed to the audience, that needs a searching discussion.

The primary use of the word "technique" is how you do the movement. And that is the main error that needs to be looked at in all modern dance and ballet in the light of scientific knowledge, so that we dancers can do more without strain, liability, and without injuries. I think the ancient metaphysical saying can be kept in mind in the training of dancers. "Only when you obey nature, nature will obey you."

Ten/ Art in Its Second Function

This essay was written for this collection, 1991.

Art in its second function is art when the artist is trying to convey an idea, or action, or mood, or something that is not literally in the material that you're dealing with—the music, dance, drama, or painting (let's leave the written word out of the question for the moment). By contrast, art in its first function is when the artist—choreographer, painter, or composer—wishes to use the wondrous aspect of art to make beautiful designs or rhythms, such as all men from the beginning of time have done, before any meaning is conveyed. You might call this art in its first function, "wondrous art." This is one of the most important aesthetic distinctions in all art thinking. It is stated in F.S.C. Northrop's *The Meeting of East and West*.[36]

Without this distinction being kept in mind, most writing about art is confused. I remember when I first came to New York from college. I was standing in the Museum of Modern Art, when it was still a brownstone front, and was listening to some people behind me saying, "But I don't understand it." I can't remember what kind of a painting it was, but it was a nonrepresentational painting (art in its first function). It was merely the painter's showing of color and shapes. It took me a long time to understand that on this level there is nothing to understand, any more than there is to understand the smell of coffee, or the texture of velvet, or the lapping of waves, or a flash of lightning. (You just sense it; you see it, hear it, feel it, smell it, and perhaps even taste it.) The rediscovery of this aspect of art is one of the bases of modern art. (Always before, in general, the criterion was to paint and sculpt to represent something that you would see. It might be a visionary thing, but the object was something as though it had existence.)

This is one of the reasons for a dance that you might call "plotless." In other words, the choreographer is not telling us anything about the meaning of the dance because there is no meaning. He is showing us the movement before any meaning has been assigned to it by the artist.[37]

Before I forget, it is useful to say that both art in its second function and art in its first function are needed, necessary, valid, and delightful. If these two functions are at opposite ends of a pole, then on the connecting line between, you'll have any work of art. Some art will be placed on the point of art in its first function and other works of art will be placed on the point of art in its second function, or a work of art can slide between the two. That has a special problem because if you go back and forth between the functions, you lack unity, and unity is one of the essential qualities of a complete work of art.

But here comes the rub. Any work of art in its second function is weak if it does not use vivid art in its first function. You can have a wonderful idea, even a spiritual idea, but do it in such hackneyed terms, that is, without vivid art in its first function aspect, that the work of art is dull, lacking in vitality.[38]

Art in its first function, before it has any meaning, can delight the eye.

Art in its second function poses a great problem. It's an aesthetic problem, and ultimately, a moral problem. (This, too, can delight the eye, but in a different way.) Art in its second function can either be life-giving or life-destroying. It might not be totally self-destroying, but even a sentence that implies that the individual is limited and can't blossom like the rose is negative and limits the universe.

When you are going to convey an idea through art, dance, painting, music, or drama, you need to be on the side of the angels and not full of despair. Everybody who is born wants to live his life abundantly. Is there anything more sad than to see children in hospitals today, born from AIDS mothers, who are going to die shortly after they are born? Look at the morning glory. The minute it is "born" it finds a way to wind its tendril around a string or another vine. Everybody who is born has it in him to go to the end of his life without being cut off.

The aim of art is to further that process of living one's life to the fullest. It can be dance, or painting, or making music, or weaving a basket, or weaving a rug, or building a house—all further life.

But here is the problem for the artist. Whenever he is trying to convey an idea to the audience, he had better be sure that it is on the side of life. Otherwise, he is destroying his life and the lives of the people who react to the art.

At this point, the artist cannot be his own man. He must convey to the onlookers some of the wisdom that the brightest men of his time, or any other time, have enunciated out of the general wisdom and knowledge of which they are capable. He has to be furthering the evolution of the race. He is a builder-upper and not a destroy-er of human happiness.

The artist must convey, in sensuous terms, the wisdom that the philosophers have arrived at (I mean not only philosophers, but all wise people whose wisdom is enunciated by being on the side of life).

One of the main errors of contemporary society is that by freeing the artist, the artist has taken over and thinks that he can originate ideas. Only philosophers can originate ideas. (Remember that philosophy is looking at your basic premises—whatever you think about life.) The artist, in this sense, is a vehicle for expressing in sensuous terms the wisdom of the thinkers. (That is why Plato, in establishing a new system for the best life in society in the new republic, tried to find out what would be the best life; whether he succeeded or not does not matter, but in one sense he did succeed, for his new republic has been a challenge to thinking about political science and even moral problems since the time of his writing.)

At this point I need to be a little autobiographical. I am eighty-two years old, and I still need reminders of how to live my life. Two years ago I did a dance called *New Moon*. I remember when e.e. cummings published *Chari*. (He lived around the corner from my apartment.) Through the years, the closing lines of his sonnet of the new moon have come into my mind every time I would see the new moon.

When the music by Lou Harrison was finished and I reacted to it, I took an image from Persian poetry of the sixteenth century, where they spoke of a young man or woman as being like a new moon. Putting those two images together, I composed *New Moon*.

But in all those years, every time I saw the new moon I was reminded of the lines:

"teach disappearing also me the keen
    illimitable secret of begin."

So here I am at eighty-two, needing, through the observation of a poet, to remind myself of how to begin again.

That is just one example or aspect of how a poet can put down in writing something that is common to all human beings, for all of us have to begin again, and he writes it with poetic vividness. Life is made up of how one approaches each day as a new beginning. But when I go down on the street and see the homeless, I wonder to myself, "Why did you not begin again?"

I believe that art in its second function, when art tries to convey a meaning that is beyond the materials for their own sake, must try to offer only life-giving messages. I can't lay down the law here. I can only investigate in my mind what seems to be useful. One of the reasons why I think our current art is in very bad shape today is because the artist, in general, thinks he's his own man and forgets that he must convey abundant life to the audience, or spectator, or onlooker.

What does one mean by life-giving art? I remember in 1960 during the first performance of *8 Clear Places* once saying to Tom DeGaetani when I came offstage, "I don't think there's a negative idea in this dance." Naturally, I certainly did not want any violence on stage, but in this case I was filled with a kind of joy and a positive emotion that the dancing had been full of life. (You would have to see *8 Clear Places* and see *north star, pine tree, rain-rain, cloud, sheen-on-water, inner feet of the summer fly, she or he snowing*, and *squash* to appreciate what I meant.)

The use of the word *sacred* in contrast to *secular* is breaking the world apart. I remember the first time I read about the American Indian idea that in general, to the Indian, everything is sacred. It means that life is all one. One of the lessons I learned from visiting the Indians of the Southwest is that all elements of nature are deemed holy. Just how far this literally, totally pervaded their culture, I don't know. But it is a point of view whereby all human activity is held in awe rather than taking a lesser view of human existence by calling some activities secular.

Once I began to hear this idea, I always felt that the making of a dance is sacred, even when it's a folk dance, or even a comic dance. In ancient Greek times (and nobody knows exactly the way it was), the Greek drama came from the worship of Dionysus and his sacredness.

Step by step, the leader of the chorus, the protagonist, and the antagonist were added. Even today, you can see the chair for the chief priest of Dionysus in the front row in the Athenian theatre beneath the Acropolis. In other words, the Athenian drama maintained its sacred character. This is all to show how the God was reborn after being slain. The net result was that the Athenian drama used the great myths from which the race evolved, and that made for a heightened consciousness and civilization, you might say even the evolution of the race.

We need delineations of the hero, examples of overcoming the negativity of the world, as in Hercules, and many other heroes. Even today, at a recent U.S. Open Tennis match, I heard someone say, "Jimmy Connors gave me courage."

What does one mean by *courage*?

The Spaniards have a name for it. It is called *Duende*. Lorca talks about *Duende*. In my feeling, it is meeting life head-on, knowing it is going to end in death, that you cannot take it with you, and yet, the flamenco singer sings praises in the middle of certain destruction. What is more powerful and touches the deep inner soul like the flamenco singer?

That also affects their dancing.

Courage in the face of disaster. Courage is the main ingredient in dance art but I suspect also in music, poetry, drama, and even painting. For most of my life I have been consciously trying, no matter how many times I have failed, to give the audience courage.

Courage seems to be the ingredient of all exciting, life-giving art. How does one give courage to the audience in seeing a plotless dance? Just to see the bodies of the dancers move with grace, energy, the very fact of being alive, that inevitable thing called a poetic sequence of movement, and rhythm showing that time is passing.

How do you show courage in a dance where you are wanting to convey a meaning, the other end of the pole—art in its second function? I think, even when illustrating or representing negative feeling or ideas on the stage, you show courage by having a moment when one says, "I see."

The great dramatic plays in general show the hero at the end of the play saying, "Now I see." King Lear, when he holds Cordelia in his arms, sees his mistake, or Oedipus, after he's torn his eyes out, says,

"Now I see." Of course there is a wide range of experience that the drama and the dance can deal with. What makes a true tragedy is that the hero, being a glorified man, ends the play by an insight.

In general, the audience needs to see some glimmer of hope at the end of the tunnel so as not to lose heart from being caught up in the negativity of the turbulent actions being revealed. Carrying this principle further, I prefer that the dancer not show a situation in which one simply wallows in despair. If you have a tragedy in drama or dance, there has to be a moment of insight.

Art, including dance art, needs to convey courage to the audience. My most recent dance, *Killer of Enemies,* stayed with me over the years, waiting for the right moment to be choreographed. Finally, I understood more. When I first undertook the dance, I intuited something more. The dance is about an American Indian of the Southwest, and the rite of how a young man finds his feeling of oneness with the world. The young man finds a way to his father, the Sun, who helps him conquer the monsters of the soul. The most poignant dialogue is where the Killer of Enemies comes back to his mother, Changing Woman, and says, "What is that red light there in the mountain north?" She answers, "Those are the gray monsters—lies, sleep, old age, hunger, and desire . . . and those you cannot kill." Then he dies, and here, the myth takes over from our common-sense understanding, and he lives forever.

This is one of the works I am most proud of. It seems to serve the function of art in its second function, of showing a prototype of how myth, which we don't understand totally, helps us live.

Our society today is suffering from a mistaken notion of how people are to be entertained and enlightened. Maybe it's at certain moments in history that people can be entertained well; such as when Aristophanes wrote his comedies, or commedia del'arte, or the comic drama in Japan, or Shakespeare's comic plays, or even the comic drama in Bali. Compare that with the gladiatorial games of the Romans and prize fighting in America where sensationalism and cruelty are uppermost in people's consciousnesses.

In Plato's *Republic,* a character, a minor character, goes from Piraeus to Athens within the long walls and then relates how he was drawn to look at the corpses that had just been cut down from being hanged, saying, "Goddam you, my eyes." Then he says, "Why did I want for my eyes to view those corpses?"

This problem about the advancement of man to peacefulness, lack of cruelty to others, and, therefore, the living of life itself with full flowering, has plagued man.

Why does man want to choose the lesser path?

Maybe there are factors that I simply cannot comprehend, but why do people in our society, at least, choose an inadequate way to live their life? By inadequate, I mean, self-destructive or full of suffering and unhappiness. Is it that they have not been metaphysically enlightened to really know how the world works? That it works through love.

Culture is a very fragile thing. Civilized life is a fragile thing.[39] It seems to me that we choreographers cannot put an image on the stage unless it has been thought through by considering what the consequences are.

I am reminded several years ago, when on television, there was a made-up story that some boys set fire to a boy of a different culture. In real life, within an observable time, there was an acting-out of the story in Boston.

The young are being taught constantly by what they see around them. If they see their families torn apart, hating one another, if they see their parents morally corrupt, that will be absorbed and will be enacted in their own lives. Likewise, if young people see men and women onstage using art in its second function to portray disharmony, these images on the stage will be absorbed and reenacted.

The artist has a great responsibility. Many times people say, "But the artist is simply reporting the time of the era around him."

I say: Art does not report its time, but it makes its time. (Art is a very great factor in the evolution of the race.) The artist is not a journalist reporting things as they are, but rather, with the wise men, the philosophers, he is "making" the time. That's why artists are chosen people. They are not concerned primarily with money. If an artist pays too much attention to money, he becomes a mere merchandiser. On the other hand, the artist needs to be paid for his work the way other good artisans and craftsmen are paid. A proper relation of the artist to his society is that he is honored for his skill and wisdom and given enough to live on to produce his art. St. Thomas Aquinas has the only rule that makes sense for an artist:

"The artist must work only for the good of the work." Too much money gets in the way; not enough money deprives the world of his useful talent. For the good artist *does have* a useful part. I have often thought, a daydream surely, if only our society could use art as, say, the Hopis in Arizona do. I felt sometimes at the end of a day of dancing at Walpi or Mishongnovi, what a unified society the dancing represented. Of course it's only a daydream. In our society, one cannot by fiat produce the correct art activity. Maybe you never can.

I have seen in the snake dance at Mishongnovi, a ninety-two-year-old snake priest leading the line that tapered off with some young boys. They were all a unity. Of course, I thought, this is thousands of years old.

Sometimes I feel the unity of society as in ancient Greece when thirty thousand saw the Greek tragedies and comedies. Today our task is to find the art process that will help bind our nation together.

This I do know. Art in its second function can be helpful by emphasizing joyous love, peaceableness, and nonviolence.

There is a wonderful saying from the Japanese poet Toju Nakae, "The natural state of man's mind is delight."

Every person in that theatre audience is awaiting a reminder of how to live with his full being without limitation. Maybe that is the reason that, over the course of centuries, nations have had temples and cathedrals to remind them of how to live their lives to the fullest, no matter that most of the time the psychological knowledge was disobeyed. The impulse was there, and that's why nations went to the cathedrals and temples—to be reminded of their civilization and civilized life every week. That is the use of the rite in theatre. It is a way of being reminded of one's civilized instincts and aspirations.

Perhaps the theatre, even the dance theatre, is the church of our time. At its most profound, it embodies the ritual of an inner life, rather than portraying the husk of an outer life. Every society needs rich metaphors of the collective insights that a culture lives by.

That is why art in its second function can create a society or destroy one. Exactly what content should go into the dance or drama I could not propose; it will come out of the collective unconscious, because it will embody the aspirations of a society.

And so, even though we don't have myths of our own today, as a substitute we can use the mythic material of other periods, as I have done in *openings of the (eye), God's Angry Man, Stephen Acrobat, The Strangler, Tightrope, The Joshua Tree, God, The Reveller,* and *Killer of Enemies.*

One of the ways that you make poetry is by the use of metaphor. When you say, "Sleep, that knits up the raveled sleeve of care," as Shakespeare does, you have made one thing stand as surrogate for another. It binds all things to everything else.

One of the dances that I did in 1952 was *openings of the (eye).* Through metaphor I hoped to get across a spiritual idea. There is nothing literal or "naive realistic" in the dance. The five sections revealed one aspect of consciousness.

It sounds rather strange to try to put the idea of the five sections of the dance into words. That is the reason why you use metaphor.

In the *Discovery of the Minotaur,* there is the consciousness that one has a problem and that one is undeveloped inwardly. One way of showing the metaphor was being bound to the floor, and therefore, not being able to move freely to solve one's dilemma. *Disconsolate Chimera* shows a wallowing around in groping for a solution of one's life. I was on a very extensive rug and I never came higher than my knees during the entire ten minutes of the dance. The ritual of the descent was a metaphor of going down into Hell as all of the mythologies show, in order to ascend again, and therefore, go in search of a solution to the problem. The *Goat of the God* shows a glimmer of enlightenment. The image of the goat conveyed the idea of just living in the moment, which is the goal of all spiritual doctrines. To make that image, I was on hooves about four inches high. I was coming to understand how the animal lives instant by instant. In *Eros, the Firstborn,* the insight arrives at the metaphor of love—the love, which pervades the world, and is available to every creature, showing the strange principle that it is there, if one recognizes it. If you don't believe it's there, it isn't. Right between my eyes, Ralph Dorazio made a representation of a third eye which I taped to my forehead. I used a metaphor of opening the third eye, the eye of enlightenment, of seeing things as they are. This is one of the great lessons that Jesus showed in the parable of the Prodigal Son, and that Hindu mythology expresses as, "Abundance scooped from abundance leaves abundance."

Another dance in which I use metaphor is *8 Clear Places.* How can a dancer dance a *pine tree?* Only through metaphor. I have danced this *pine tree* since 1960, and every time I come back to it, I see what a wonderful metaphor it is, and how bold; but it works. As I have danced it, I have felt that all of the movements metaphorically registered pine tree. There was nothing choreographically that I could do to "naive realistically" represent a pine tree. It had to be by metaphor. The richer and more inventive the metaphor is, the greater the poet, like Shakespeare. How does a choreographer tell that the metaphor works? That is poetic intuition. That's what makes a poet—the poetry of the dance.

The great part of the success of the metaphor comes from the costume. I have a very wide red sleeve for one arm, with a black leotard, and a green legging on one leg. For the face, Ralph Dorazio made an abstraction of pine needles, but they are in no way "naive realistic." The pine needles are arranged on a stick of wood that I tie to my face.

Here again, I developed the metaphor for *rain-rain, cloud, sheen-on-water, the inner feet of the summer fly, she and he snowing,* and *squash.*

Another dance in which I use metaphor is *Black Lake.* Even the title is poetic, for *Black Lake* means the night sky. In the same way as dancing pine tree, how can a woman dance the setting sun or the first star, or two nightbirds, or convey the effect of a comet? When it comes to the clouds that go over the moon, one dancer holds the moon like a fan in one hand and two other women with plain square tissue paper weave back and forth over the moon.

In similar fashion the dancer, using the metaphor of thunder, enters on stage with two black panels on the front and back of his body. In the section using the metaphor of the big bear and the little bear in the night sky, I brought in a humorous idea. Even their masks have a little representation in them because they are bears. The last section, *The Milky Way,* is one of my boldest inventions. How can a group of dancers dance the Milky Way? Only through metaphor. The dance happens to be a startling example of the disparate elements that startle meaning in the metaphor. Without its mysterious alchemy, there is absolutely no aliveness, and very often, absurdity rather than communication. A disparate element in *The Milky Way* is a long entrance with the dancers facing the back, making a stamping noise in the silence. The use of metaphor belongs to "poetry"—the poetry of any art—painting, music, and of course, word-poetry. Anna Kisselgoff, critic of the *New York Times*, has called my use of metaphor my greatest achievement.

We have lived, in the last seventy years in America, in one of the great dance cultures of all time. Never have so many people danced as an art. I think it is going to be one of the remarkable things in the history of the world. Some great pioneers of the human spirit were opening up new paths of consciousness, from Isadora Duncan to Ruth St. Denis and Ted Shawn, and Loie Fuller, on to Doris Humphrey, Charles Weidman, Hanya Holm, and Martha Graham. Even a large part of their main activity was evolved within a few blocks of where I'm writing.

Whether this great flowering is going to die or whether it will consolidate itself by the second generation of dancers into new works of art that are going to aspire to a more complete and total work of art is the question. That is why there is great work to be done by new choreographers who are going to aim at uplifting the consciousness of people in America.

Will this glorious art come to its full blossom, or will it die?

It seems to me that the dance art can bind our people together and show the great promise of this nation, unique in the history of the world in creating a country (which we easily take for granted) where every man is permitted to have his own religion.

That was a tremendous achievement. Now, modern dance has the opportunity to add a new dimension of freedom to human consciousness around the world—the lovingness of an aesthetic aim—embodied by the free and living work of art. Only when people come to the point of seeing and experiencing life's goal aesthetically do they ever become truly free and happy.

Only when we have developed our aesthetic sense will we have a culture that doesn't miss the boat. When we value the creation of art in its first function (its pure sense of delight) and when we can use art in its second function in a non-neurotic (not self-destructive) way, then we will all share in the fullest, richest meaning of life.

Notes

1. Arch Lauterer, known for his spare, clean-lined spaces, was a set designer who worked with Martha Graham. In the 1930s he designed a dance theater for Bennington College that was never used. Subsequently, the Martha Hill Dance Workshop, a dance theater designed by the architectural firm Robertson Wourd of Chicago was opened at Bennington in 1977. (David Scribner, Director of Public Affairs, Bennington College, telephone interview, August 1991)

2. [For Hawkins, the dance *Bluebeard* lacked maturity, Ed.]

3. The term "avante-garde" has been misused and ruined in ten years' time. The self-indulgence of the "avante-garde" so-called artists of 1970, I repudiate.

4. Harald Kreutzberg (1902–1968, Czechoslavakia) studied with Rudolf von Laban and Mary Wigman. Appeared in solo concerts of his own works and with Yvonne Georgi (his principal partner) and Ruth Page. He danced in the United States through the 30s and 40s.
   Yvonne Georgi (1903–1975, Germany), choreographer and ballet mistress, studied with Dalcroze, Wigman, and Victor Gsovsky.

5. By "the revolution" I mean the change in the last part of the nineteenth century and early part of the twentieth century.

6. Kathakali (literally, "story-play") represents a whole range of Hindu literature. Actor-dancers are generally young men. Costumes and make-up are stylized. Pantomine gestures are characteristic; body movements are descriptive.

7. Arthur Joyce Lunel Carey (1888–1957) is best-known for his two trilogies about social and political changes in England. The last novel in his first trilogy, *The Horse's Mouth*, is the story of the visionary painter Gulley Jimson.

8. Northrop, F.S.C., *The Logic of the Sciences and the Humanities*, (New York: Meridian Books, 1959).

9. Laban, Rudolf, *Modern Educational Dance*, (New York: Frederick A. Praeger, 1963), p. 56: "In an action capable of being stopped and held without difficulty at any moment during the movement, the flow is bound."

10. Ibid. "In an action in which it is difficult to stop the movement suddenly, the flow is free or fluent."

11. Rochlein, Harvey, *Notes on Contemporary American Dance*, (Baltimore: University Extension Press, 1964), p. 15. Rochlein uses the phrase "Theatre of Perception" to characterize a human quality of

dance that doesn't depend on emotionalism to evoke a response, but strips movement of everything but its poetry to find the essence of expression.

12. Lincoln, Kirstein, "What Ballet Is About: An American Glossary," 1 (Winter 1959): 6.

13. Marcuse, Herbert, *Eros and Civilization,* (Boston: Beacon Press, 1966), p. 183.

14. Ibid., p. 189.

15. Ibid., pp. 186–187.

16. Brown, Norman O., *Life Against Death,* (Middletown, CT: Wesleyan University Press, 1959).

17. Northrop, F.S.C., *The Meeting of East and West,* (New York: The Macmillan Company, 1946).

18. Marcuse, *Eros and Civilization,* p. 183.

19. Ibid., p. 189.

20. Rochlein, *Notes on Contemporary American Dance,* pp. 26–27.

21. Northrop, *The Meeting of East and West,* p. 407.

22. Laban, *Modern Educational Dance,* p. 56.

23. Ibid.

24. *Measure for Measure* 2. 1. 223. "Truly sir, I am a poor fellow that would live."

25. R.H. Blyth is the author of *Haiku* and other books. The specific reference for "All that can be shaken . . ." was not found.

26. Pirsig, Robert, *Zen and the Art of Motorcycle Maintenance,* (New York: Ballantine, 1975).

27. "Ma Muse, Ma Mort," is a quote by Jean Cocteau (1889–1963). It refers to his contention that the poet must die several times in order to be reborn, a thought expressed in his 1950 screenplay "Orphée."

28. Jacques Maritain (1882–1973), French Neo-Thomist philosopher, opposed the modern tendency to disown the proper function of reason. He regarded the metaphysics of existence—the study of being—as the highest expression of human intellectual activity.

29. Sisyphus, in Greek Mythology, is the son of Aeolus and founder-king of Corinth. Zeus consigned Sisyphus to eternal punishment in Tartarus, his sentence being to push a great boulder to the top of a steep hill perpetually. Albert Camus used this legend in his essay, "The Myth of Sisyphus," as a metaphor for man's fate.

30. "Flirt of a bird's wing" is from a poem by the American poet Parker Tyler. The exact citation could not be found.

31. *The Tempest* 4. 1. 155. "And, like this insubstantial pageant faded."

32. Northrop, with great brilliance, shows that everyone has "Trapped

Universals." A Trapped Universal is a shorthand form for delineating this dance idea: Bad patterns of movement, once ingrained, will remain until such time as the knowing dance teacher shows one how to get rid of them. Northrop shows that children assimilate information from parents, teachers, playmates, et al.; these ideas can either be right or wrong both on a physical-material level, and the psychological level. If the individual makes deductions from this later on in life, he may be making erroneous deductions, if his first information was wrong. He doesn't know that he is making these deductions from his first premise. But if the premises are wrong, the deductions will be in error.

It behooves the teacher to try to eliminate from the student's mind the erroneous pattern from the past. If the lower back is contracted tightly, it will limit all movement; the teacher's job is to identify (and sometimes it takes a long time) those practices that prevent the full range of movement, and thus reduce the possibility of injury.

33. The word "strain" means a lack of harmony that one wants to avoid in the engine of his automobile, in a bank statement, in the relations between a father and son, in the workings of a political system, or as demonstrated by Charlie Chaplin in *Modern Times* when he attempts to eat corn on the cob via a machine.

34. This common error in ballet theory has its equivalent in the life of ordinary people. Tightness in the lower back is the most common ailment in the general population.

35. "Excenteredness" means moving a leg, an arm, or even the trunk farther from center than the movement actually requires. All movements that are efficient and graceful are always enfolded around the center of gravity.

36. Reprinted by Oxbow Press, P.O. Box 4065, Woodbridge, CT, 06525.

37. If the painter or dancer happens to evoke some image that you might see in the outer world, he does not mean for that to be paid attention to. It takes a certain sophistication to be able to look at a dance or a painting and not see it as "naive realism." For example, if I, as a painter, make a configuration that looks too much like a face, when I don't mean for it to be a face, I would say that is inept art. But sometimes audiences and critics see a "naive realistic" object where the artist could not have possibly intended one.

Unsophisticated onlookers of painting and dancing very often boil everything down to its "naive realism," just as in poetry reading there are always some teachers who want to eliminate the poetry, the indefinable phrasing, and just read the plain sense as we everyday speak it. How can you tell the plain sense of this?

> "Full fathom five thy father lies;
> Of his bones are coral made;
> Those are pearls that were his eyes;
> Nothing of him that doth fade
> But doth suffer a sea change
> Into something rich and strange.
> Sea nymphs hourly ring his knell . . ."
> *The Tempest* 1. 2. 397–403.

The same thing can happen in dance. The poetry of the dance is something you can't boil down to its plain sense.

One of the problems of interpreting dance is that the artist may have included, and in such a manner that he's not entirely conscious of it himself, a poetic meaning. The dance can mean something but nobody can quite SAY what it is. That is what I might call the poetry of any art, or at least one aspect of what is meant by poetry.

38. One of the great works of art in our time is Picasso's *Guernica*. In its second function the painting depicts the Hitlerian bombing of a Spanish town during the Spanish Civil War and shows all of the suffering and destruction that resulted. But what makes this an extraordinary, great painting is that all of the elements of art in its first function are extremely vivid. You might say that Picasso invented a new language of painting, one that eschews "naive realism." Even some of the slight distortions of the figures make the art in its first function more lively; you wouldn't say shocking, but more full of intense drawing.

39. The Spanish philosopher, Ortega y Gasset, having realized that the population of the world had doubled, possibly tripled since the Napoleonic Era, reached this conclusion: "The young have not had time to be taught."